I Dare You

Yes you can

Blaine

Win the Debate in Your Own Head

Think before you act. Before you undertake any major task or challenge, think it through. Imagine what the perfect outcome will look like. People are forever trying to decide what to do best to survive or to get advantage.

You have the power to make a negative out of a positive or a positive out of a negative. Even in an emergency there is time to do good thinking. You can decide to do nothing, you can decide to do something or you can decide what will enhance the chances that you will achieve your perfect outcome.

Before you act, first win the debate in your own head.

Eagles Dare

They have been admired for centuries for their ability to see far, to soar high, to overcome adversity and to strike when the opportunity arises.

Images of eagles are used on national flags and by governments and religions and on family coats of arms to symbolise power and freedom.

Some eagles are carnivorous, others are vegetarians. Most birds gather in flocks. Eagles tend to go solo and set their own agendas. They have their own definition of success that's right for them.

They dare to seek their own opportunity. They focus on their objectives and go after them. Then they become role models that other eagles follow.

I Dare You

Win the debate
in your own head

Blaise Brosnan

MANAGEMENT
RESOURCE
INSTITUTE
(WEXFORD)

Production

Editor: Michael Freeman

Production Editor: Helen Ashdown
Wordswork, Clonleigh, Palace, Co. Wexford

Design and Layout: Rosbui Media, Wexford

First Draft Reviews: Brendan Cahill-Flynn, Margaret Hawkins,
Declan Lyons, Celestine Murphy and Paddy Whelan

Printing: Swift Print Solutions Ltd., Rathnew, Co. Wicklow

Distribution: Gill and Macmillan, Dublin.
ISBN 978-0-9934650-0-0

DISCLAIMER

This book offers personal information and guidance only and is not intended as direct advice. The author and publishers have no control over the way that the reader uses information contained in these pages. The reader has sole responsibility for the outcomes of any actions, he or she takes.
This book is a valuable guide. However, it is recommended that the reader always employs qualified professional specialist advice.

My thanks to my wife, Delia,
my daughter, Caitriona and her husband, Barry,
and my son, Pádraig, and his wife, Anita
and son, Tadhg, for their support.

Acknowledgements

I have a number of heroes in my life. They are my inspiration. Some have known tough times and have overcome those tough times to live well and grow.

The people who made this collection possible are the many people I've met on my journey.

I would like to record them all but there wouldn't be enough space in which to do so.

Blaise Brosnan

Thousands of people in many countries of the world including the USA, Europe and Russia and his native Ireland have been influenced by Blaise Brosnan as an educator and a trainer.

Blaise Brosnan is former chief executive of a business which he helped to build from a tiny entity to a turnover of many millions.

Photo: Gerard Hore

He founded his own management consultancy and business training enterprise, the Management Resource Institute (MRI), more than 25 years ago. Since then he has helped transform the lives of thousands of people and the turnovers of many businesses working with individuals, government bodies, SMEs and major corporations.

He is a graduate of University College Dublin (UCD) and of Trinity College Dublin. He is founder-director of International Dispute Resolution (Ireland) Ltd. He was a board member of the world-famous Wexford Opera House, now Ireland's National Opera House, during its multi-million euro development.

His first book, *You are the limiting factor – Unlocking your True Business Potential* (2009) and his second book, *Jack – Business Lessons from Life, Life Lessons from Business* (2011) have become class bestsellers.

Books by Blaise Brosnan

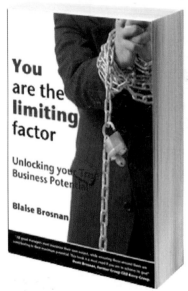

Blaise Brosnan's books *Jack – Business Lessons from Life, Life Lessons from Business* (2011) and *You are the limiting factor – Unlocking your True Business Potential* (2009) have received critical acclaim in local and national media.

What they say about Blaise Brosnan

"An amazing man…"
Brendan Howlin TD | Minister for Public Expenditure and Reform

"This is one of the most practical books on business skills that you are likely to come across – buy it, more importantly, use it."
Dr Sean Mythen | Former CEO Wexford County Enterprise Board

"All good managers must maximize their own output, while ensuring those around them are contributing to their maximum potential. This book is a must read if you are to achieve this goal."
Denis Brosnan | Former Group CEO, Kerry Group

"Success in business begins with the individual. Ultimately, self-belief, emotional resilience, discipline and unrelenting personal commitment drive business performance. Blaise Brosnan's book is full of insights and nuggets of wisdom."
Paul Hennessy | Partner, PricewaterhouseCoopers.

"Managing your career has always been important, but I believe it is even more essential in today's very uncertain world. Blaise in his book *You are the Limiting Factor* gives very practical advice in helping you develop your career by both challenging and guiding you on your career path. This book could help you reach your optimum potential in business"
Philip Lynch | Former CEO of One Fifty One plc.

"He continues to influence us as our mentor, critic and advisor."
Rachel Doyle, Arboretum Lifestyle and Garden Centre, Leighlinbridge, Co. Carlow

Be Authentic – don't try to be someone or something you are not. Instead value yourself and the impact you can have. Life is much more fun that way. Use some of the nuggets within this book by Blaise to facilitate you on this journey.

Cathriona Hallahan | MD Microsoft Ireland

Blaise Brosnan is sharing a lifetime's learning and experiences that will change how you think and act in all areas of your life. Up there with Rhonda Byrne's *The Secret*, I dare you to read this book and achieve the success you desire in your personal and professional life.

David Walsh | MD Netwatch

There are many more losers than winners in the entrepreneurial game. It takes courage, vision and faith to believe that you can be one of the 5% of those who succeed in turning their dream into reality. For the 95% it becomes a nightmare that exists primarily in their own heads. The hard-earned experience shared by Blaise Brosnan is spot on. It is also timeless – as valid 50 years ago as it would be today – or when we're all just faded memories. In short, easy-to-read essays he gives some masterful lessons in strategy. Think through the big picture, only do what you believe in and passionately enjoy the ride! I love the wisdom. We all have so much to learn from '*I Dare You*" – the entrepreneur's handbook.

Jerry Kennelly | Founder and CEO, Stockbyte, Stockdisc and Tweak

For a Kerryman who claims that he cannot tell a joke, Blaise Brosnan can communicate his business theories through simple stories. I found his lectures to be stimulating and motivating.

Marie Fenlon

Blaise Brosnan came into our lives a few years ago and things have never been the same. With his gentle manner, practical no-nonsense approach to business and years of practical experience, Blaise has helped us on our journey to success. We have a long way to go, but knowing Blaise is at our side gives us the confidence to continue. I cannot recommend Blaise highly enough.
Margaret Kirwan | Director at Goatsbridge trout farm

Blaise Brosnan is porridge for breakfast. He provides a constant slow release of inspiration, skills and tools that energises every day.
Anna Wickham

We'll never look at rocks, monkeys or elephants in the same light again.
Wicklow LEO Class

If you need help in starting-up a new business, or re-energizing an existing business, you won't find a better mentor.
Hugh Ivory

He never judges you. Instead he encourages you and puts success within your reach.
Josephine O'Hagan

A hotline to a pillar of savvy common sense.
Claire Goodwillie

Blaise, thanks for saving my bacon. I will be forever grateful.
Eavan

Many thanks for all of your excellent advice. You can be assured that it was all taken on board. One of your final slides – 'If not now, when?' – was an excellent way to sum it all up.
Anthony

Contents

ARE YOU SUFFERING
ENOUGH RIGHT NOW
TO WANT TO CHANGE
OR WOULD YOU RATHER
WAIT UNTIL YOU
FEEL WORSE?

Change is good for you

Walking along Curracloe beach one summer, I saw a huge wave come in from the sea. Children playing nearby had created a sandcastle. The wave destroyed the sandcastle, flattening it there on the beach. The children were dismayed. After a few minutes, when they restored their calm, they changed the scene. They dug down and created a space in the sand.

What was once the site of a giant sandcastle became a play-pool and the children played there welcoming with great excitement every other big wave that crashed down on the beach and into the play-pool they had themselves created. Their crisis became their opportunity.

A metaphor for life is a giant tapestry or patchwork quilt. Each patch is interwoven with the other. Each patch is held together with the other by knotted threads. Where is your current patch? Where are you headed? Which knots do you need to untie and redo in a different way?

The journey of life is filled with scenes and experiences. The journey keeps changing as we drive along. The dynamics of life change in type and intensity depending on what stage of life we are at and heading towards.

There are many things we cannot control on the journey. At a macro level, the weather and the government and the rest of the world may be beyond our control right now. At a micro level, inside our own homes, our own workplaces, our own communities and our own minds, there are many things we can control and from which we may influence the future for the better. Our reaction and follow-on actions to the issues and events around us right now decide and determine our future.

You will often feel uncomfortable and challenged in life. That is good. If you are planning to sit at the same desk or stand at the same workbench for the rest of your career, you will need updated education and new skills to adapt to change. That is good. Stability can be good but change too is good. Change is vital for survival and for living an enriched life.

People have thousands of small victories or mini-successes every day. I believe we should focus on those mini-successes. Even though we may fail often, we must try to multiply our mini-successes and create our own opportunities.

In my life so far I have watched many people fail and I have watched many of them rise again to achieve success. I have watched opportunities appear and I have watched people fail to take those opportunities within the lifetime of the opportunities.

I have gathered hundreds of messages of wisdom from those people, from my own heroes and from my own experiences over my lifetime and I have collected them in this personal collection. I hope they inspire you. I hope in particular that they help you to identify and make the most of your own opportunities.

I now invite you to come on a journey of purpose with me, guided by experience and fuelled by passion. Be prepared to be influenced and become a positive influence on others along the path.

Blaise Brosnan

How to use this book

Regard this book as a companion and friend. Keep it on your desk, in your pocket or in the car or wherever else you might want to reach it. Open a page anywhere at any time. Each message has implications for you. It may inspire you, may console you, and may guide you. You may adapt the messages to generate your own philosophies of life and living.

Reflect on just one message at a time. Throughout the book I have interspersed a number of what I consider to be powerfully inspirational pieces from my own personal collection of poetry, verse and viewpoints gathered from some of the great philosophers and thinkers over a lifetime. They continue to influence me. I hope that by presenting them to you here in this gift-book, you too will experience positive wholesome influences from them and that you will in turn give them to others.

While we are influenced by others, we, too, are influencing others. By reflecting on some of the messages within this book you will be better equipped to be a good influencer. You can become a better influence on the people around you or the people with whom you come in contact.

We are, all of us, each of us, on a journey. By reflecting on the messages, you may be inspired to enjoy the journey no matter what challenges you encounter along the way.

Messages for life

This book is all about you.

You

are an important person ...

... an immortal diamond ...

... a unique and amazing creation.

Please take some time out. Relax for fifteen minutes. You deserve it. Sit down. Have a cup of tea or coffee or better, a glass of water. Breathe in for six seconds. Hold your breath for three seconds. Exhale for six seconds. Do it ten times.

If you've been working hard, or are under stress, you should take a break every few hours. Medical friends of mine say that every hour, you should get a ten minute break! Get up from your desk, get out of the car, get out of the van or juggernaut, get off the tractor, stretch, and go for a quick walk.

While you are taking this break, I want to talk to you. You can take it or leave it. I have something that may be of value to you. You may learn lessons from the following pages that will help you cope with problems no matter how big. You may learn something that will help you understand, become aware, trigger another thought, make you better off or even rich, whatever your definition of rich is. You may want a new car, a house, a holiday, education for the children or to put food on the table. You may simply wish to be healthier or to just simply live for the time you have.

I have drawn on my own experience growing up in a small rural area in Co. Kerry, going to national school and then to university, working in the USA, the UK, Middle East, Asia, Russia and Wexford and studying the lives of many experts who have been through the life process. I have collected the sayings and statements in the book from several people I've met over the past fifty years. Their wisdom is in this book.

I like to see someone cope with whatever life throws at them, survive, grow in health and in small victories over adversity and achieve whatever they want to achieve. You should not stretch yourself beyond your capacity to stretch. On one hand, you might be amazed at how fragile you are or how sensitive you are to one adverse move. On the other hand, you might be amazed at how powerful you can be and the influence you have.

While you are sitting there, just imagine what life would be like if you had everything you needed and wanted. Imagine that instead of working harder for it, you might achieve it by working smarter. You might stretch yourself just to your capacity over a long period of time.

No matter what you have been told before, there's a price on everything. You'll have to pay for it upfront or you can defer payment until you can more easily afford it. It may be money. It may be your time. It may be your pride or dignity. It may be the giving of your own experience or wisdom. This is tough but realistic. Are you prepared to pay the price? I want you to pay as little as possible in the long term. I would like you to work but work smarter than you have ever worked before. I would like you to grow.

This book provides messages that provide signposts on the road along the journey to your destination. There are no direct roads to that place. It is inevitable that you will go down some cul-de-sacs. You may want to stay in a cul-de-sac or you may, without satnav or map, using only your own innate resources, wish to know how you will get back on the main road again.

Be aware that you may get a breakdown now and then. You will be tested to what you perceive is beyond your limits. Sometimes the wind will blow in your face, or from the side, but hopefully more often to your back.

I wish you an interesting and profitable new journey.

Your opportunities

You are made up of your DNA, your inherited genetic map, your experiences and how you have reacted to the influences, opportunities and threats you have encountered this far along your life's journey.

You can't do anything to change your DNA. However, you have a choice on how to react to the opportunities and threats facing you from this moment forward.

The world keeps changing. The dynamics of life keep changing. The formula that you used for success in the past may no longer work.

Every new journey starts from where you are now. To complete the journey, read the messages in this book and reflect on them. Be inspired by the sayings of the wise.

Meanwhile, keep your destination in sight. Don't forget that you have a major influence on those you meet along the road.

Some of the messages in this book will leave you uncomfortable and challenged. That's good. They may be the catalyst for you to leave your comfort zone and move towards your new destination. Now, take your first steps forward based on purpose and fuelled by passion.

First steps

I f you are in Kerry and you want to get to Dublin, you can get there by car, plane, train, and bicycle or by walking the full distance. It would make no sense to walk all the way as it would cost you valuable time and you just might miss some great opportunities.

To get from Kerry to Dublin will cost you time and energy and money, but you must weigh up the costs versus the opportunity. Perhaps you are happy enough where you are and don't want to take the journey at all. That's okay, too, if that's where you really want to be. Before you decide, think that you are going to miss out on meeting some amazing people along the way; you are going to miss some beautiful scenery and you are going to miss some wonderful opportunities.

If you are in New York or Beijing or Dubai and you want to get to Kerry, the best way is probably by a combination of a taxi and plane. Either way, the journeys to Dublin or to Kerry are not direct. They are not in straight lines. You may have to use different methods to reach your destination. Chances are that if you follow a tried and tested itinerary, walked by many others before you, you'll get there more easily and earlier than they did.

Similarly with life. When you set out on the journey of life it will not be in straight lines. It will rarely be as the crow flies. You have a number of options. You can take the long way or the shorter way, the faster way, the least expensive way or the scenic route. Here are my three signposts to success:

Step 1 – Start at the end

Before you set out on any journey or do any task it is a waste of time, energy and money to go without thinking and planning. The best place to start is at the end. What is the destination? What do you want to achieve? Where do you want to get to? That position on your satnav, that village, that profit on your accounts, that education, that personal objective, is always at the end.

Next, decide how you are going to get there. Get a map. Do some research. Imagine with all your heart that you have reached that destination. Create a clear picture of it in your mind. When you have completed that exercise you will be already half way along the journey. I'll tell you later about planning, faith and persistence and about completing the journey.

Step 2 – Dream

There is a challenge. Where precisely is the destination? You can think up your destination as you think best at present in your present circumstances. You will probably adjust your destination the more clarity you get later on. You can begin to define your destination by some dreaming, some imagining, perhaps some scribbling and doodling.

Try to dream and doodle. You don't need to be able to write precisely, or draw precisely. You can change all that later. Take a sheet of paper and a pen or pencil or colour pens. Draw a circle, a rectangle, a triangle, write out all the letters of the alphabet, write out from 1 to 10 several times, write a tot of a few figures. Draw a flower, a tree, a dog, a car, a house, a plan. Draw anything that comes to mind. All on one page. That should get your creativity and thinking processes going.

Step 3 – Keep going

A bicycle will remain upright if you keep pedalling it forward. You can speed it up or slow it down while still keeping it upright. If you stop pedalling, you'll stop. Keep pedalling at a certain speed so that you can adjust to going along the flat, up hills and down hills and over rough terrain in all weathers. You will do it more easily the more often you do it.

Cycling, like brisk walking, can be good for your general health and well-being. Medical professionals tell us that it is good for you physically and psychologically, good for your cardiovascular system and releases endorphins. You'll feel great. If cycling, you will need to take some precautions. You will wear a helmet to protect you in case of accident. Cycling is a wonderful metaphor for travelling the journey of life. Sometimes you'll need to get off the bike, take a rest, gaze at your surroundings, look at your compass and revise your journey.

In order to keep your bicycle upright, stop thinking about your age. It's only a number. People grow old when they have abandoned their purpose in life. Decide your destination or your purpose in life and then keep on pedalling in its direction. Stop every now and then for a rest.

In life, if you don't have your own plan, you will be vulnerable to the plans of others. So, when you have decided your destination, set out your own plan to get there. Your challenge will be to stick to the plan that you now set. Will you stick to it? Will you be blown off course by some emotional change of heart or will someone else, or some outside force, change it? If so, will you be able to get back on track or change course?

Life Phases

Defining moments on your journey

MESSAGE 1
CHILDREN

Listen to children

Thirty years ago I watched a little eight-year-old, fun-loving boy run up and down the driveway of his home creating imaginary swoops and dives in the air with the toy aeroplane that he held in his hand. His father and mother, both from so-called working-class families, both with no background or interest in aviation or aircraft, encouraged his fantasy. He carried his interest in aeroplanes into his teenage years. When deciding his career at the age of seventeen he had only one aspiration – to become a pilot.

In law, a child is a child up to the age of eighteen

Parents can learn from children

Trust is the glue that binds children to parents

Anon

Q How many children would you like to have?

Today, he is an airline captain flying huge passenger planes across the world. He loves aeroplanes and he loves life. He credits the love and encouragement and support of his parents for helping him to realise his dream and for his present fulfilling life.

Children are gifts of God, amazing creations, the future custodians of the world. Their fathers and mothers are their primary carers. They have a huge responsibility to ensure that each child is nurtured and grows into a responsible, caring, achieving and coping adult.

Youth is not entirely a time of life; it is a state of mind. It is a temper of will, a quality of the imagination and vigour of the emotions

Anon

Nothing makes a child as smart as having grandparents

The only time in our lives when we wish to get older is when we are children. If you're less than ten years old, you're so excited about ageing that you think in fractions. 'How old are you?' 'I'm four and a half!' You're never thirty-six and a half. You're four and a half, going on five!

Anon

Parents wishing to achieve change in their child should first check if it is something that could better be changed in themselves

*Communication is
a two-way street.
Listen hard to better
understand the
issues as children
understand them*

Change yourself
and, by the Law of
Reflection, the child
will adapt

A little girl in a
refugee camp
responded to a
television journalist
who sympathised
with her that she had
no home. She said
that she had a home
but that her parents
just didn't have a
house to put it in

Anon

Contrary to what many parents think, teachers are secondary, perhaps only supplementary to that care when children reach school-going age.

The critical years in the development of the child are those between the ages of two and seven years when children learn through their senses. At roughly aged seven they learn to reason and think. By the age of ten or twelve they develop awareness of the world at large and take greater interest in others.

Communication is vital to ensuring that children develop to their utmost potential. The profile of children will be influenced by the genetic map that their parents give them together with the influence that every other person, grandparent, sibling, uncle, aunt, cousin, friend, neighbour, teacher has on them. To communicate with children, listen to them.

Q: What are you going to do differently? How are you going to do it?

Think about this ...

Children
learn what they live

If a child lives with criticism, he learns to condemn.

If a child lives with hostility, he learns to fight.

If a child lives with ridicule, he learns to be shy.

If a child lives with shame, he learns to feel guilty.

If a child lives with tolerance, he learns to be patient.

If a child lives with encouragement, he learns confidence.

If a child lives with praise, he learns to appreciate.

If a child lives with fairness, he learns justice.

If a child lives with security, he learns to have faith.

If a child lives with approval, he learns to like himself.

If a child lives with
acceptance and friendship,
he learns to find
love in the world.

Dorothy Law Nolte

MESSAGE 2
TEENAGERS

Become an anchor and a rock

A school principal in charge of a major secondary school in Dublin told me that the most important and the most challenging time for parents is when their children become teenagers. Pre-puberty and adolescent years are a time when children need more care from their parents than when they were four, five or six years old. Teenagers will deny this, but subconsciously they are asking parents to be their anchor and their reliable reference point and often their rock during the transition from child-hood to adulthood.

Teenagers will tend to live up to or down to your stated and unstated aspirations and judgement calls about them

Give the young person a fine reputation to live up to and they will try to live to it

Q How many years would you tolerate a troublesome teenager for?

Children cannot choose their cousins but they can choose their friends

The best careers advice to give to the young is:
'Find out what you like doing best and get someone to pay you for doing it'

Katherine Whitehorn

Parents and peer groups have a huge influence on the fast evolving teenage boys and girls soon to be young adults. Peer groups in particular have a major influence on them.

When teenage boys and girls are rebellious or are free to do as they please, they usually try to imitate each other. Because of this, peer-group influence will try to crowd out the positional power of parents. Teenagers are trying to define their own independent path in life. They shift their reference points from their parents to the other teenagers with whom they associate.

This is a time for parents to build bridges with their teenage children and it is a time for parents to help them understand that there are consequences for their decisions and follow-on actions. It's a time for teenagers to learn that everything has a price tag. There is a price for doing and there is another price for not doing.

It's a time for parents to become their rock on which they can rely for their safety and stability and it's a time for parents to become their anchor to haul them back to reality and their reference points and values in life when required. Those are turbulent years for most teenagers as they adjust physically and emotionally to major change in their lives that will impact on their behaviour as adults.

Teenagers need true friends with whom they can be sincere, think aloud in their presence and let their guard down completely. It's not easy for a parent to build the relationship of friendship and trust with a growing teenager. Parents might start with catching their teenage children out in acts of courage, acts of initiative and acts of kindness and give them genuine heartfelt praise.

Parents know that for their children, home is not necessarily where they live, but where they feel understood.

Q How can you relate better to your teenager?

Think about this ...

Memo from a child to parents

• Don't spoil me. I know quite well that I ought not to have all I ask for; I'm only testing you.

• Don't be afraid to be firm with me; I prefer it, it makes me feel secure.

• Don't let me form bad habits; I have to rely on you to detect them in the early stages.

• Don't make me feel smaller than I am; it only makes me behave stupidly "big".

• Don't correct me in front of people if you can help it; I'll take much more notice if you talk quietly with me in private.

- Don't make me feel that my mistakes are sins; it upsets my sense of values.

- Don't protect me from consequence; I need to learn the painful way sometimes.

- Don't be too upset when I say "I hate you"; sometimes it isn't you I hate but your power to thwart me.

- Don't take too much notice of my small ailments; sometimes they get me the attention I need.

- Don't be inconsistent; that completely confuses me and makes me lose faith in you.

- Don't forget that I cannot explain myself as well as I should like; that is why I am not always accurate.

- Don't nag; if you do, I shall have to protect myself by appearing deaf.

- Don't put me off when I ask questions; if you do, you will find that I stop asking and seek my information elsewhere.

- Don't tell me my fears are silly. They are terribly real and you can do much to reassure me if you try to understand.

- Don't ever suggest that you are perfect or infallible. It gives me too great a shock when I discover that you are neither.

- Don't ever think it is beneath your dignity to apologize to me. An honest apology makes me feel surprisingly warm towards you.

- Don't forget I love to experiment. I couldn't get along without it, so please put up with it.

- Please keep yourself fit and healthy. I need you.

MESSAGE 3
ADULTS

Stand for something

John F Kennedy, Martin Luther King, Nelson Mandela and Mother Teresa stood for human rights and better life and living. So, too, have thousands of people who will never be acknowledged or achieve fame.

It doesn't matter if you are rich or poor, what religion you are or if you are of no religion, what political party you support, what football club you follow, what pop star you worship, what music you like, what clothes you wear or what beer you drink. However, it does matter that, as an adult, you stand for something.

When you become an adult you acquire extra legal responsibilities and social responsibilities. Everybody has moral responsibility. Governments and society impose legal responsibilities. You form your own moral and social

Any fool can complain or condemn, and most fools do

Blame looks back, responsibility looks forward

If you don't stand for something you will fall for anything

Q What would you do if you had no worries?

responsibilities from your values and your moral code derived from your family background, culture, philosophy, religion or school.

I assume that imperfect though they may be, you respect the laws of the land and that you try to live by the cultural and ethical codes and practices that control civilized society. I assume that you would behave peacefully in the company of others. I assume that you stand for and will campaign for improvement in the quality of life and living for your family members, your friends and for members of the community around you. I assume that you will help someone who needs help and that you will defend someone who is being attacked.

I assume you stand for something.

If you view your problem closely enough you will recognise yourself as part of the problem

Q: What are you going to do differently? How are you going to do it? When will you have it completed? What evidence can you give to show that you have made the sustainable change?

We would be happier with what we have if we weren't so unhappy about what we don't have

Frank A. Clark

If you think you are average, you will achieve average results

Stretch yourself, but not beyond break-point for your health and happiness

Here are some suggestions:

I stand for democracy

I stand for human rights - the right to privacy, the right to dignity

I stand for equality in gender, in race

I stand for reward for work

I stand for justice and for fair play

I stand for honesty and truth

I stand for integrity

I stand for the opportunity to provide for myself and for my family

I stand for the opportunity to make money

I stand for freedom of expression

I stand for freedom to choose whatever religion I like

I stand for reaching out, sharing and helping others.

You may have other ideas, some differing ideas or some that are similar to the above. Every idea, every thought, is a valuable resource.

What do you stand for? Stand for something.

We don't see things as they are; we see things as we are

Anais Nin

Sometimes it is not good enough to do your best; you have to do what is required

Winston Churchill

Nobody grows old merely by living a number of years. People grow old only by deserting their vision and principles

Q Are you prepared to pay the price?

Personal Management

From good values to great habits

MESSAGE 4

MOTIVATION

Get out of your comfort zone

The only one who can tell you "You can't" is you. And you don't have to listen

The more I want to get things done, the less I call it work

Efforts and courage are not enough without purpose and direction

John F. Kennedy

Just imagine winning a million in the National Lottery. If you knew in advance that you would win a million you would probably walk across a bed of hot coals to buy a lottery ticket. You would be motivated to get out of your comfort zone.

We humans are natural goal setters. However, we fail to achieve most of our goals because of a lack of motivation. Most of us prefer to stay in our comfort zone. The easiest way to get us out of our comfort zones is to become motivated for our own reasons. The hard way is for somebody else's reasons.

My best friend is the one who brings out the best in me

Q Are you ready to stretch yourself by taking on a meaningful challenge?

MESSAGE 5
PERSONAL

Become passionate with purpose and persistence

Passion, n: enthusiastic interest; an expression or outburst of feeling; ardent love.

Purpose, n: power of seeking a desired end; a definite intention.

Persistence, n: to continue steadfastly or obstinately especially against opposition.

Those dictionary definitions describe the intangible conditions or states of mind that drive survival, success and the path to a new way of living. Another condition that is allied to them is Resilience – the ability to bounce back despite adversity.

What are your expectations for each of those close to you?

If you want lasting success, create a life that matters to you and you will find that it's difficult to retire from the obsession

A task becomes hugely burdensome or even unpleasant if it is not fired by passion, determined by purpose and aided by persistence. I have met thousands of people who have mediocre talent but great passion and I have watched them succeed more than those who are advantaged and have great talent left dormant. The challenge brings out their abilities. They keep driving onwards. They persist. They are bothered until they succeed.

The most successful people that I have met in my work are passionate and persistent. They have won the debate in their minds about what they want to achieve. They have a clear vision and they hold on to this vision with focus and with determination.

If you want lasting success, create a life that matters to you. Become passionate about the development of yourself, your family, your work, your interest, your health, your hobby, the project that you are working on.

It may seem to be a paradox that you can be your true self and your commercial

> We grow not by what is given to us but by what is expected of us

> A person can succeed at anything for which there is enthusiasm

Charles M. Schwab

> Real success is when you live your life in sync with your value system

self at the same time but, yes you can. They are zones or modes or ways of thinking and acting that you can enter, adapt to and leave as the need arises or the changed situation requires.

Victor Frankl, the Austrian psychiatrist and author of *Man's Search for Meaning*, endured and survived several notorious concentration camps including Auschwitz and Dachau in Nazi Germany during World War II. Despite his terrible ordeal, he kept his purpose to keep on living. He grew his own identity from little and won the hearts of his captors and his guards. Until his release by the Americans in 1945 he persisted for more than two years of captivity as his true self and with purpose, passion and persistence to achieve freedom.

With your feet planted on the ground, use your eyes to survey beyond your reach. You decide the elasticity of this reach

Persistence makes the impossible possible, the possible likely and the likely definite

Q What are your expectations for yourself one year from now?

Think about this ...

Letting go

Be prepared
to let go,
if you want
to facilitate
change. You can
do it provided
you want to
do it badly
enough.

There's nothing to fear – you're
as good as the best
As strong as the mightiest, too
You can win in every battle or test
For there's no one just like you.

There's only one you in the world today
So nobody else, you see
Can do your work in as fine a way:
You're the only YOU there'll be.

So face the world, and all life is yours
To conquer and love and live
And you'll find the happiness that endures
In just the measure you give.

There's nothing too good for you to possess
Nor heights where you cannot go
Your power is more than belief or guess
It is something you have to know.

There is nothing to fear – you can and you will
For you are the invincible you
Set your foot on the highest hill
There's nothing you cannot do.

MESSAGE 6
MIND

Visualise the outcome

Henry Ford, genius, motor car inventor and manufacturer whose grandfather and father came from Cork, famously said: 'If you THINK you CAN or THINK you CAN'T, you're right.' What you think about all the time has a good chance of becoming your reality.

What your mind thinks, your body acts on to prove that your mind is right. Act on what you think to make things happen. But, before you act, consider your options.

We have no right to ask when a sorrow comes 'Why did this happen to me?' unless we ask the same question for every joy that comes our way

Philip F. Bernstein

Visualise the outcome you desire. Create it in your mind

The mind is its own place and in itself can make a hell of heaven and heaven of hell

John Milton

Commitment achieves completion

The top achievers in business, politics and sport who are challenged to achieve change or goals, use an imagination technique called 'Visualise the Perfect Outcome'. They imagine the goal or the outcome that they desire.

We become what we think about. Every good idea and every bad idea comes from that few square inches between your two ears – your mind. Your thoughts translate into emotions and feelings, most of which you can manage yourself.

Enthusiasm is the fuel of accomplishment

As a man thinks in his heart, so is he

The Bible

Praise means approval

Win against yourself

Q **What would you do to achieve anything you want in life?**

MESSAGE 7
HABITS

Crowd out bad habits with good habits

A friend of mine would scratch his head every time he spoke on the phone. He broke this habit by snapping an elastic band on his wrist when he found himself repeating it. He then reached for a pen and notepad to jot down key words from the conversation. He cured himself of the habit and gained from the experience.

You are an accumulation of your habits built up over the years. From how you get out of bed in the morning, how you shower, how you dress, how you walk, sit, talk, how you respond to the world, how you act in front of others, and how you think. You're living out your habits.

In a law firm that I visited, three staff members were in one staff room which had computers and printers and client files and other paraphernalia

He who treads softly goes far

Chinese Proverb

Motivation is what gets you started. Habit is what keeps you going

Jim Ryan

that law firms have. Every few minutes a staff member would stand up from her desk and race down a long corridor to photocopy a sheet of paper, bring it back and put it into a file. It is doubtful that there would have been a health benefit to staff by running in stress mode from the office down a corridor to the photocopier and back. Simple ergonomic solution: move the photocopier closer to where it is needed. The irony of the case is that the manager of the law firm had intended to move the photocopier to the main office five years previously. She procrastinated. Running down the corridor to the photocopier became a habit. Over years, it cost time, money, stress and hundreds of wasted miles.

Good habits are a constructive and economical way of performing your normal role. Habits are necessary. They free up your mind so that you can concentrate on how to survive day to day. Most habits are stored in your subconscious, waiting to be called upon. You don't have to think about how to drive your car so you can be on the lookout for danger while you are driving. You don't have to think about how to walk. This allows you to concentrate on where you're going.

You develop your habits by going through a stepped process from being unconsciously incompetent, to being consciously incompetent, to being consciously competent to finally being unconsciously competent.

Are you a creature of habit, repeating an old formula that is no longer effective or efficient, but doing it quicker and sweating more? New research has indicated that it takes the average human about thirty days to develop a new habit. Some take less, some take more. Habits are the outward manifestation of your thoughts and attitudes. They are your greatest enablers. They can be your greatest inhibitors.

Ninety-five per cent of the things you do are regulated by your habit. You acquire habits over time as you learn to survive in this ever-changing world.

Unfortunately, habits can also keep you locked in self-destructive patterns which will limit your success. To become successful, crowd out bad habits with new habits which are in line with the life you want to live.

Where are your habits leading you? If you could flip your habit-coin and do the opposite, what would be the implications for you? If you ate healthy meals, exercised and got enough sleep? If you stopped procrastinating? If you socialised with enablers? If you delayed current consumption for future gains?

Fear of the unknown is the biggest obstacle to breaking your habit. Habits are broken by substitution of one habit for a more satisfying one. Consciously recognise the new habit is giving you more satisfaction.

We are what we repeatedly do. Excellence is not an act, but a habit

Aristotle

If you would persuade, appeal to interests rather than intellect

Benjamin Franklin

Q Can you write your own mini action plan that replaces three old habits with three new habits?

MESSAGE 8

VALUES

Be true to yourself

I n *The Field*, the acclaimed play by the Kerry writer, John B. Keane, the Bull McCabe said to Tadgh, 'Isn't it better to have our principles than be millionaires. God made the world, but we made the field.' The values of the Bull overshadowed the values of legal ownership and led to conflict and bloodshed. That was the price of principle and the result of being faithful to personal values.

Your values are your core beliefs and priorities in your life. They are the hidden guiding rules that direct your decisions and your actions. They are your subconscious 'learned behaviours'. You are not born with them. You acquire them as you live and interpret all of your actions and reactions to issues as they arise. If you want lasting success and happiness, create a life that is yours.

> It's never too late to become what you really want to become provided it is right for you
>
> *George Eliot*

Q What do you NOT have to motivate yourself to do?

Synchronise your planned journey with your values and your life will be simpler and more fulfilled. Your mission must be what is right for you rather than the fulfilment of someone else's agenda. There is a higher longer-term price to be paid if you are not living in harmony with your core values. You are living in harmony with your values when you are engaged in work that taps your talent and fuels your passion. You've got purpose fuelled by passion.

What are your value expectations of yourself? Specifically the challenge for you is: 'Can you be both your real self and your commercial self, while still being true to your core values?' The answer is: 'Yes, you can, if you are prepared to learn to adapt to each situation as it requires.'

Are you a paradox existing in a contradiction? Why are you doing what you are currently doing? Are you working in your present job for approval? If so, for whose approval? Is it for fear of being disliked? Is it because of guilt? Is it for other reasons?

The late Nelson Mandela, former president of South Africa, said that he had to pay a big price in order to achieve his public successes. Part of this price was his twenty-seven years in prison and two failed marriages. A friend of

One man cannot do right in one department of life, while he is occupied in doing wrong in any other department. Life is one indivisible whole

Mahatma Gandhi

It is a greater compliment to be trusted than to be loved

George MacDonald

mine expressed his paradox in this way: 'I have achieved material success and all the perks. Yet why is my life so empty compared with my mates who have so little and yet seem so contented?'

Many people seem to have achieved outward success but are internally at war with themselves. Stars of stage and screen and captains of industry are associated with glory and contentment. Instead they may have short-term glory and longer-term addictions and unhappiness. They may have achieved their professional goals but at the price of their personal and family lives. Get-rich-quick guys from a lower class try to acquire happiness by buying into an upper class.

Talented careerists sell their bodies and their minds to their corporate commercial masters. Instead of being called prostitutes they are called captains of industry and success stories. Thousands of public and civil servants are in jobs that inhibit their creative talents or their wish to be entrepreneurs in private industry. They may be living in their own prison. Is there much difference from being jailed for life?

You will create your own success formula if you discover what is most important to you and plan your life based on your values. When your head is clear, put in place an action plan to make it happen. Your answer and follow-on action to these questions provide the secret for your future success, as you define success. That success is defined by you.

Q Do you want to live rich and die poor or live poor and die rich?

MESSAGE 9

GOALS

Look to the top of the mountain

John F. Kennedy expressed his wish in May 1961 to achieve the impossible. He said: 'This nation should commit itself to achieving the goal, before the decade is out, of landing a man on the moon and returning him safely to earth.'

Eight years later, on July 20, 1969, astronauts Edwin 'Buzz' Aldrin Jr., Neil Armstrong and Michael Collins boarded Apollo 11 and turned his dream and his goal into reality. Neil Armstrong and Buzz Aldrin became the first two individuals to ever land on the moon. It was in Armstrong's words, "... one small step for man; one giant leap for mankind."

Without a goal, you are like a ship without a rudder

The ripest apples are on the high overhanging branches. You may trip if you reach beyond your arm's length

Everyone needs goals. Everyone needs a sense of direction. To reach the summit of a mountain, first face the mountain and secondly, take small steps in its direction. By setting specific goals or objectives for yourself you are more likely to achieve what you want.

Big goals can be subdivided into mini-goals, each achieved one at a time, each a step on the path to the bigger goal. You can set personal goals, family goals, business goals, community goals.

How to set goals is a challenge for most people. Goals should be SMART – Specific, Measured, Achievable, Realistic and Timed. First, imagine or visualise precisely what the goal is. Second, write down a detailed description of the goal. Third, estimate how much better you will be when you achieve your goal if it is realistic. Fourth, set a time-limit by which to achieve it.

Your goals help you to plot your desired future. They must be followed with actions. It's the possibility of your goals coming true that makes life exciting. Do you want to continue dreaming about your goals, or do you want to use them as enablers to helping you live your dream?

Goals without plans are merely aspirations. Goals without deadlines are merely dreams

If you can find a compelling reason, you can do it

Some people make things happen, some watch while others make things happen and some wonder what happened. Which one of these characters are you?

Without written goals, you will lack purposeful direction. A lack of direction can be disorientating and frightening to the point where you are just spinning on the spot and gaining no traction to move forward. Write your goals on paper. Amend them if you need to.

Choose goals that truly represent your values and desires. Your time is limited, so don't waste it living someone else's dream. Base your goals, and their underpinning action plans, on issues which are right for you. In other words, your goals must be synchronised with your deeply held values. When you perform in line with your values, you will experience an inner peace of mind. This will facilitate you to become passionate about it.

If you have a big enough 'Why?' you can bear almost any 'What?' or 'How?' When your 'Why?' is big and exciting enough for you, you will find a way to reach your targets. You may have to struggle and try many different tactics to get there. Don't lose sight of your 'Why?' as expressed in your written goals.

Start to take the necessary steps towards your goals. Every journey starts with the first step. Failure to get beyond the start stops most journeys

People with written goals succeed because they see where they are going

If you have accomplished all that you have planned for yourself, you have not planned enough

Edward Everett Hale

Keep your goals high enough to inspire you and low enough to encourage you

Your long road forward is a series of little journeys. Monitoring your progress through each little journey allows you to make the necessary adjustment to your overall roadmap on the way to your big goal.

A successful vision creates a tension caused by both the activities of your right creative and left logical brain. This tension will give you the necessary energy to lead-out your necessary change.

If you don't know where you are going you will probably end up somewhere else. The Law of Attraction indicates that if we are clear about where we are going, we will attract to us the means of making it happen.

Q What is success for you? What gives you meaning as you see it?

More men fail through lack of purpose than lack of talent

Billy Sunday

You see things; and you say 'Why?' But I dream of things that never were; and I say 'Why not?'

The serpent in Back in Methuselah *by George Bernard Shaw*

Not failure, but low aim, is a crime

James Russell Lowell

MESSAGE 10
TIME

Kill procrastination

When asked to give an opinion on the subject of time, Saint Augustine said: 'If nobody asks me, I know; but if I wanted to explain it to someone that should ask me, I do not know.' Benjamin Franklin said: 'Don't squander time for it is the stuff life is made of'; Napoléon Bonaparte said: 'Take time to deliberate, but when the time for action has arrived, stop thinking and go in'; John Adair said: 'Look in the mirror and you will see your biggest time waster.'

Time is a valuable but perishable resource. Everything we aim to do requires time.

If only we could waste less time on the things we don't want and use time more on the things we want, we'd be happier.

I have watched people whose concept of timekeeping is to clock into their jobs on time

Good managers never put off until tomorrow what they can get someone else to do today

Procrastination is the thief of time

If it wasn't for the last minute, nothing would get done

every morning and to clock out on time every evening. Their concept of productivity is to 'be there'. There are many people in bureaucracies who are stifled by 'the clock-in-clock-out' regime and who wish to be free to use their time as they wish.

I have met many entrepreneurs and owner-managers of business organisations for whom there is not enough time in the day. They are under continuous pressure to meet objectives or deadlines but they love the challenge. In the creative professions, severe time constraints can be destructive. In manufacturing, time management and productivity is crucial. For parents, the battle for time is continuous. For children, time is forever.

If you want to get more quality time for yourself to do the things you'd like to do, do the tough things today. Stephen R. Covey, author of the *Seven Habits of Highly Effective People,* advises you to put the big rocks into the jar first. Then you'll get the pebbles in! Do first things first. Get the business of the day done in the day if you can.

Worry is wasting today's time cluttering up tomorrow's opportunities with yesterday's troubles

Few notice what has been done; they see what remains to be done

We cannot manage our outer environment until we manage ourselves better. The first step is by changing our attitude to the monetary value and usage of time

You can't do everything on your own. You won't have enough time. Delegation is an interactive process of empowering someone to deliver your outputs. Most people are not good at delegating. They don't understand the difference between delegation and abdication. They shy away from calculating thc opportunity-cost. They tie up their own scarce resources and do it themselves. Successful people owe much of their greatness to their ability for effective delegation while maintaining control.

Build your business by outsourcing the operational links of the chain. A 'home-baked' cake doesn't necessarily have to have been baked in your home.

It's easy to decide what you're going to do. It's hard to figure out what you're NOT going to do. Decide what has to be done, who will do it, when it has to be done and how it should be done. Think of what not to do, who shouldn't be selected to do it, how not to do it and when it's too late to deliver.

There is a clear distinction between effective delegation and abdication. If your use of time is not rational there is no point in seeking marginal improvements by just managing the time slots.

Most output happens just before the important meeting not after. What gets measured gets done

Don't let yesterday take up too much of today

Will Rogers, 1879-1935, cowboy, actor, philanthropist

I not only use all the brains I have but all I can borrow

Woodrow Wilson

By doubling your time on the 20% that gives you the most value you could probably work a two-day week and achieve 80% more than your likely current output. Productivity could be doubled by halving the amount of time for its completion.

You will not be working to the 80/20 rule if you go along with the crowd. Instead, focus on the inputs which advance your measurable outputs.

To make the most of time usage and to kill procrastination separate effort from reward. Know that hard work doesn't necessarily lead to optimum results. Give up feeling guilty, have a timed mini plan that you'll stick with until it becomes a habit and focus on your targeted outputs. Flip the coin from input to measured output.

Worry can become fear

FEAR is Fantasised Experiences Appearing Real. As your mind loses control, issues that are small can take on a life of their own in your head and crowd out the more important and vital big issues. The antidote to worry is purposeful action

What is worth doing is worth the trouble of asking somebody to do it

Ambrose Bierce, 1842-1914

We must use time wisely and forever realise that time is always ripe to do right

Nelson Mandela

Q Can you identify an occasion where you might abdicate rather than delegate?

Think about this ...

Take
Time

Take time to laugh;
it is the music of the soul.

Take time to think;
it is the source of power.

Take time to play;
it is the source of perpetual youth.

Take time to read;
it is the fountain of wisdom.

Take time to pray;
it is the greatest power on earth.

Take time to love and be loved;
it is a God-given privilege.

Take time to be friendly;
it is the road to happiness.

Take time to give;
it is too short a day to be selfish.

Take time to work;
it is the price of success.

MESSAGE 11
DOING

Nibble at the unmanageable

People live life by doing. We never stop. The challenge of doing many things makes life interesting. Life throws up challenges to keep us going. Some say it's God's attempt to make us better. If you don't exercise your muscles, they'll weaken. If you don't stretch your mind, you'll never learn.

If you are faced with what seems to be an insurmountable problem, I assure you that there are millions of people just like you at this moment.

You may think you have only two options in dealing with a challenge: 1. Go through it or 2. Go around it. Instead you may have four options: 1. Do nothing. 2. Nibble forward at it. 3. Delay it to another, perhaps better, time or 4. Delegate it.

While God gave us the ingredients for our daily bread, he expected us to do the baking ourselves

If it's right, do it and if necessary, look for permission later

Many people believe that if you focus long enough on the challenge a creative solution will arrive.

How would you eat an elephant? The answer is 'in bite-sized chunks'. With any major challenge, take time out to think its size and impact and consequences. Break it down into its bite-sized chunks, in other words, its component parts. Nibble at it, but in a forward direction.

If you are stuck in a comfort zone, get out of it. What would happen if you were to break the cycle of doing things as you have done them all of your life up to now? Would you be better off to break that cycle?

What are the five most critical issues facing you at present? What action plans are you prepared to put in place to address them? How can you manage the variables you have control over? Write your problems down on paper and redefine them until you achieve clarity.

Follow your passion rather than your pension. You cannot wait for satisfaction to come into the future

To optimise your potential stretch yourself

Be honest enough with yourself to understand your current base so that you can more sensitively experience the "niggling-need" to change it. Otherwise why go through the pain of change?

The way to get started is to quit talking and get doing. Every change-journey starts from the point you are at right now

You can't direct the wind but you can adjust your sails

since you may not live long enough for it to happen. Pay the price in order to energize your passion. It may be difficult but it's possible. Since most of us are in our comfort zones, it is generally easier to stay put rather than change.

You are where you are based on the decisions you made in the past. Your future positioning will be based on the decisions you make now and into the future. Are you really open to change? Are you open to doing something about it right now?

Some people shoot first at something and whatever they hit, they call it the target. The better approach is to look first for the target. To get to the top of the mountain, start climbing from the foothills. Begin somewhere. You cannot build a reputation on what you intend to do. Live and succeed within the enabling and hindering forces out there. Take

Every great achievement was once impossible

Before you decide to take on something new, decide what you are willing to let go. Are you prepared to pay the price?

Take advice from professionals who know what to do, how to do it and when. However, it's up to you to do it

The one who says it can't be done should never interrupt the one who is doing it

You cannot have a different output if you do not change your input

Enthusiasm reflects confidence, spreads good cheer, raises morale, inspires associates, arouses loyalty and laughs at adversity. It is beyond price

Allan Cox

responsibility for your choices. It's the only way you can liberate yourself from the conditioning of your life journey to date. Wishing for something to happen is a start. Until you do something about it, nothing will happen. Try nibbling at the unmanageable with the objective of freeing up your time and energies for a better future and getting to the next phase of your plan.

Wisdom is knowing what to do next. Skill is knowing how to do it and virtue is doing it

David Star Jordan

We judge ourselves by what we feel capable of doing while others judge us by what we have already done

Henry Wadsworth Longfellow

Ninety-nine per cent of failures come from people who have the habit of making excuses

George Washington Carver

Q Can you identify a big task in your life right now and break it down to a stepped action-plan on paper? Do it and monitor progress. Celebrate the victory.

MESSAGE 12
ACTION

Do it now

eak performers have more than goals. They have a vision of what their life will be like after achieving their goals. They do not live in the future but they make sure that each step taken in the present keeps them on the road toward their goals.

How you act today, based on the lessons of yesterday, will help decide the outcome of tomorrow.

There are two days in the week upon which you cannot worry. Yesterday, with all its pluses and minuses, is gone. Tomorrow, with all its possibilities, is as yet unborn. It isn't the experience of today that drives us mad. It is the remorse of what happened yesterday and fear of

People may doubt what you say, but they will believe what you do

If you have a feeling that the present can be improved, innovate

No success or failure is necessarily final

Execution of any new idea or strategy is the ultimate challenge

what tomorrow might bring. The best time to do something worthwhile is between yesterday and tomorrow. That time is now.

Strive to keep your promises. Reallocate your time to more important things and avoid hurry and indecision. Address the big issue that's bothering you. Apologize if you need to and move on. Get your affairs in order. Remind yourself that you are human and to not demand perfection of yourself until you are perfect. Understand who is most important in your life and tell them how you feel now.

The past is history. The future is mystery. Now is a gift. That's why now is called the present.

Do it now.

Great spirits have always encountered violent opposition from mediocre minds

Albert Einstein

There is nothing more difficult than to take the lead in the introduction of a new order of things

Niccolo Machiavelli, father of political theory

Think like a man of action, act like a man of thought

Henri Bergson, French philosopher

Q What is stopping you?

Personal development

Growing up, growing wise

MESSAGE 13
EDUCATION

Empower people through education and training

Thomas Davis, barrister, writer and founder of *The Nation* newspaper, born in Mallow, Co. Cork in 1814, famously said: 'Educate that you may be free.'

The Department of Education in Ireland nobly sets out general aims of primary education: to enable the child to live a full life as a child and to realise his or her potential as a unique individual, to enable the child to develop as a social being through living and co-operating with others and so contribute to the good of society and to prepare the child for a continuum of learning.

The same aims might be applied to adults. Empower people through education and

We are always in the education process as we experience the University of Life

Curiosity is the driving force in the movement towards knowledge

training. Encourage people to engage in a continuum of learning.

People must learn to grasp new concepts and information to keep up with the pace of change in society. They must be taught to assimilate facts and ideas; how to research and plan; how to notice trends; how to put up arguments and counter-arguments and explanations; how to quickly develop relationships with others; how to quickly identify what is relevant and how to solve problems.

Experience may not be enough to allow people to reach their potential and personal fulfilment.

Education transmits knowledge and skills, helps create an enterprise culture that in turn creates jobs and drives economic growth. Education and training play a critical role in creating necessary change in society.

Education shapes the thinking of people so that they become independent, take initiative, feel responsible, become aware, know and understand how to live well, how to

Education may appear to be very expensive but you should try ignorance

Knowledge is power. Education empowers

Ability is the power to apply knowledge to practical purposes. It is being able to close the knowing-doing gap

Ignorance of the present and ignorance of the future are pardonable but ignorance of how ignorant we are is unpardonable

promote change and create better societies and better standards of living.

The best businesses and professional associations provide for continuous professional development and improvement through mandatory attendance by employees at training courses every year.

You can decide what you want to become. A good education and training to acquire specific skills will facilitate you to achieve this objective.

Problems and issues cannot be successfully solved with the same thinking that got you there in the first place. Humans can change their lives by changing their attitude and how they view issues. Education has a critical role to play in empowering people.

Q Are you open to learning more?

Do not walk behind me, I may not lead. Do not walk in front of me, I may not follow. Just walk beside me and be my friend`

Albert Camus

Great minds must be ready not only to take the opportunities but to make them

C.C. Colton

Success or failure is caused more by mental attitude than by mental capacity

Sir Walter Scott

The best of all things is to learn. Money can be lost or stolen, health and strength may fail but what you have committed to your mind is yours forever

Louis L'Amour

MESSAGE 14
WORRY

Focus on opportunity

Eckhart Tolle, in *The Power of Now*, invites you to live in the present moment and to avoid worry and anxiety about the past or the future. Dale Carnegie says: 'Shut the iron doors on the past and future. Live in Day-Tight Compartments'.

Worry is common among people today. It wastes today's time and it crowds out tomorrow's opportunities with yesterday's troubles. It is compounded by negative emotions or feelings that paralyse and often overwhelm. Such negative emotions include anger, guilt, jealousy, self-pity, feelings of disappointment, loss of dignity and so on. Continuous worry can cause stress and chronic stress can kill.

 A condition of living and participating in today's society is that you feel worried. The art of worrying people is now an industry. Through the post, email, the telephone, the national

Today is the tomorrow I worried about yesterday

Most of the things you worry about never happen

Concern is useful but worry is a waste of time and of life

Adversity may provide you with advantage

media and social media, come warnings and reminders about the bank, bills, the car, the electricity, health, bad news, loss of job, loss of business, deadlines for tax returns and so on. Ads on television, the radio and in newspapers and magazines also feed on insecurities.

The positive response to fear is to face it and act. The negative response is to avoid it, shy away, postpone it, and deny it, just kicking the can down the road.

Part of the worry condition is that, as a child, you may not have been able to distinguish between valid and invalid criticism. 'You are lazy.' 'You are a bold child.' 'You are useless.' 'You are not as good as Mary or Joe next door.' These are messages that may have been programmed into your sub-conscious by unenlightened parents or by teachers under the influence of the then culture.

When my team and I worked in Tula in Russia, we met a beggar on the street. She was initially aggressive but she calmed down and then revealed herself to be an articulate and well-educated lady. She said: 'You Westerners think you know it all.

The view from the outside in is different from the view from the inside out

Your attitude will determine the actions you take to overcome adversity

Be true to yourself

You come here and prescribe for us. You are looking at us from the outside with your Western values. I see a different world from my side.'

One of the lessons that I have learned in life is that our perceptions about the circumstances of others is generally wrong.

There is a danger that you will build a comfort zone around one or a combination of negatives. There is a further danger that you will build an identity around them. An antidote to this condition is to try to reduce the time you spend blaming others and past circumstances for your current condition or circumstances. This is what economists call the Opportunity Cost of not doing something.

Recall some recent issues that you were worried about. Did the worst actually happen? What did you do about it? What do you want to achieve within the next twelve months? What mini-action plan will you commit to making it happen?

Beat worry with purposeful action. Don't worry about failure. Be concerned about the chances you miss when you don't even try. Focus on the opportunities that await you.

Wants that are far beyond your means or capacity lead to unhappiness

It takes self-confidence to be happy in your own skin and be guided by your own agenda rather than by your neighbour's status symbols

Q What would you do if you had no worries and knew you could win?

FEAR

Think about this ...

From "If"

"If you can keep your head when all about you are losing theirs and blaming it on you...

If you can meet with Triumph and Disaster And treat those two impostors just the same.

Rudyard Kipling

Face fear with action

Stress, worry, anxiety, panic, sensitivity, and fear are parents, brothers and sisters. Worry and continuous fear can affect your health. Chronic stress, an outcome of continuous worry, can kill.

Only about ten per cent of the things we worry about happen in the way we visualize. If only we could isolate this ten per cent.

I complained because I had no shoes until I met someone who had no feet

Worry tends to grow in intensity when you have too much time on your hands. It's a form of negative objective setting – whatever you dwell upon grows. You vividly imagine the negative outcome when you worry. Be careful about what you visualize. Influenced either by the positive or negative focus of your mind, it has either a nasty or a happy possibility of happening.

When you move beyond your fear you are free. Some fears should be respected but most of them are irrational and a hindrance. Everything is relative and so are your fears and their accompanying stresses.

The antidote to fear is purposeful action. The reason this antidote works is because of the Law of Substitution. You cannot worry about something if you are working

People stumble over pebbles, never over mountains

Anon

Q Can you isolate one thing that is causing you stress? Write it out on paper. Then attack it in a structured way, driven by purpose and passion to take care of it by managing yourself with more clarity and measuring your progress.

If you can't sleep, get up and do something instead of lying there worrying. It's not the lack of sleep that gets you – it's the worry.

Doubt arises because of a perceived lack of information or certainty. Dispel it by gathering facts.

Accepting responsibility helps to give you control and freedom. If you continue to make excuses, you are in reality running from your responsibility and you are losing control over your forward journey. You are responsible. Take control. Too much freedom can represent no freedom.

At work the great majority of people tend to focus downward. They are occupied with efforts rather than results. They worry over what the organization and their superiors "owe" them and should do for them. And they are conscious above all of the authority they "should have". As a result they render themselves ineffectual

Peter Drucker

Think about this ...

Don't you quit

When things go wrong as they sometimes will
When the road you're trudging seems all uphill
When the funds are low and the debts are high
When you want to smile, but you have to sigh
When care is pressing you down a bit
Rest if you must, but don't you quit.

Often the struggler has given up
When he or she might have captured the victor's cup
And he or she learned too late when the night came down
How close he or she was to the golden crown
Success is failure turned inside out
So stick to the fight when you're hardest hit
It's when things seem worst
that you mustn't quit.

Anon

Personal leadership

Making things happen

MESSAGE 16

MARRIAGE AND PARTNERSHIP

Communicate

Sinéad Caulfield, a young woman of 35 and her husband, Pádraig, live in Dublin and have two children and a third on the way. Sinéad said their lives are a never-stopping rollercoaster. Work and living and marriage and babies and stress leave them with little time for recreation. They have a mortgage on their three-bed semi-detached home and they have a loan for their cars. They rush from home to crèche to work and back again. They say they are stretched to their limits with their loan and mortgage repayments. They have rows and disagreements and yet fall in love all over again. They say they are healthy, they have jobs and they say

Happiness is when A has something that B lacks and B something that A wants

Never marry for money, you will borrow it cheaper

Respect your partner. Otherwise both of you are travelling on different journeys

Marriage is like going down the Niagara Falls in a canoe-race. Some will land in a still pond. The rest will have to paddle like mad to survive

Respect is oil that takes the friction out of living together

Q What can you do today to improve your primary relationship?

they are lucky compared to their friends. In their own minds, they are living in bliss.

Molly Murphy died this year aged 96. Throughout her life, she was in her own mind a young woman of 21, the age that she met and married Jack. She was besotted with Jack who pre-deceased her by fifty years aged 46. She continued to love her memory of him for the rest of her life. She doted on her three children, her daughters-in-law and son-in-law and grandchildren. They in turn loved her deeply.

Molly's philosophy for marriage was: have respect for each other no matter what happened in the ups and downs of life, support each other, acknowledge each other's differences and complementarities, and give each other independence.

Sinéad and Molly represent an 'ideal' type of marriage. Their communication levels have kept them on their journey. Their key to success is that they create undisturbed spaces for their togetherness. Let there be spaces in your togetherness.

Many couples live outside of their ideals. Some continue and endure 'dysfunctional' marriages for life.

People fall in love, want to live together, enjoy each other physically and emotionally, and share their interests and lives. In Western societies, marriage is based first on the idea of romantic love. Many couples regard marriage as restrictive. They prefer to live in partnerships that are free of the legal framework of the traditional marriage system.

In some societies, the marriage is based on the property or commercial value or class of each of the partners. There have been thousands of 'arranged' marriages built on the belief that romantic love or like of each other will develop as the journey of life unfolds for partners over many years of living together.

Most people begin their marriages and partnerships happily. However, in living together for some time, their behavioural, personality and opinion differences become evident and clash. Every marriage gets tiresome or boring at times. Some marriages break down irretrievably which may be good for both partners in the long term. It is human and it is natural that people are attracted to each other, fall in love and seek personal and sexual fulfilment. It is also human that many marriages and partnerships fail.

Marriage or partnership for the long term is not a destination – it's a journey that every day reveals new scenery and new experiences. Whatever the background and cultural differences of the partners, good communication is key to positive relationships, sexual intimacies, resolving differences and keeping the family, however constituted, together for the journey.

To plough the field, the horses work side by side

MESSAGE 17

OPPORTUNITY

Start anywhere, start anytime

Opportunities are like buses – miss one and there'll be another along soon

Take the opportunity of a lifetime within the lifetime of the opportunity

Bill Gates might never have achieved anything had he not taken the opportunities of his lifetime.

Opportunity is defined variously as the time or circumstance in which you can achieve something. Buy that car, that dress, that toolbox right now or you'll pay more for them later. Go golfing and you'll miss the TV programme. Do that training course and you'll have the opportunity to get a promotion and a salary increase. Now that you have got that inheritance or windfall you have the opportunity to build a new house or go on a holiday.

The opportunity may present itself. Adversity can create opportunity for great achievement.

Taking the opportunity or not is your decision. Or you may create your own opportunities.

Perhaps you can set up a business and take the opportunity of the upturn in the economy or the growth of a new niche market or service. Of course you may consider the opportunity cost – the cost of taking one opportunity but not another. Your opportunity is probably here and now.

Start anywhere. Start anytime.

Nothing lasts forever. One's strategies need to keep changing. In the 1940s sex was relatively safe and flying was relatively dangerous. In the 2000s flying is relatively safe and sex is relatively dangerous. In our lives and business we have to keep redefining ourselves.

Q What can you start today by phoning someone?

One person's loss may be another's opportunity

There is no security on this earth – there is only opportunity

It is not what happens to you but how you react to it that matters

There is no limit to what can be accomplished if it doesn't matter who gets the credit

Ralph Waldo Emerson

Every opportunity has a difficulty, and every difficulty has an opportunity

J. Sidlow Baxter

Think about this ...

F.W. Woolworth

When young F. W. Woolworth was a store clerk, he tried to convince his boss to have a ten-cent sale to reduce inventory. The boss agreed, and the idea was a resounding success. This inspired Woolworth to open his own store and price items at a nickel and a dime.

He needed capital for such a venture, so he asked his boss to supply the capital for part interest in the store. His boss turned him down flat. "The idea is too risky," he told Woolworth. "There are not enough items to sell for five and ten cents." Woolworth went ahead without his boss's backing, and he was not only successful in his first store, but eventually he owned a chain of F. W. Woolworth stores across the nation.

Later, his former boss was heard to remark,

"As far as I can figure out, every word I used to turn Woolworth down cost me about a million dollars."

MESSAGE 18

FORWARD AND UPWARD

Embrace the future

During life we are faced with many watershed points, twenty per cent of which are critical. The decisions we make about which road to turn onto at these critical points have a massive bearing on our lives.

Going from the known to the unknown is always frightening. It involves a stepped process of disengagement from the old way of doing things and becoming excited about the new possibilities. The most difficult decisions are tackling your sacred cows. These are the people and assumptions that you consider to be immune to change.

If you want truly to understand something, try to change it

Kurt Lewin

The incremental approach to change is effective when what you want is more of what you have already got

Richard Pascale

Before you decide to take on something new decide what you are willing to let go. You cannot keep frontloading your life without off-loading something.

Business people at stage one of their business cycle often make decisions intuitively since they still lack the breadth of relevant experiences. Almost every opportunity seems to be a priority. If you haven't been careful at managing your business through this potentially fertile stage, you may have fallen into the trap of trying to go in too many directions at one time.

Be careful about stretching your scarce resources and talents too thinly. You might run out of working-capital and a major trading set back might be the end of the business.

As issues, opportunities and emergencies emerge, you have a choice about how you react. Be positive. Take time. Give the emerging issue or opportunity or emergency due consideration and then decide.

If you are unprepared, your tendency will be to hunker down, be defensive, cut costs and eliminate people. This may not be the best approach at a time of significant opportunity to improve your position in your market place.

We should not let our fears hold us back from pursuing our hopes

John F Kennedy

Another option may be to adopt two contra tactics. One tactic is to make a major transformational change. The other is to make small incremental changes.

A series of "little" changes, known as the Kaizen way of gradual, positive change, can be effective. The Kaizen way may be counter-intuitive since you might think that you need big new steps. Because it involves a sequence of smaller steps it's more difficult to see the results compared with the results from transformational changes.

But inches make champions. There are only inches or split seconds between the winners of the gold and silver medals in the Olympics. Operating the Kaizen way through small steps seriously reduces the resistance and fear factor associated with change. Nibble at it.

Business success is not about getting individual bits of your business right. It's about how you get the total process working together in an integrated way so that the value of the synergy is optimized. If your behaviour is to have impact, change your attitude so that your new approach becomes a habit. Embrace change and your future with enthusiasm.

No inspiration is worthy until someone takes action to make it work

Anon

Q If there was one change that you should make in your life right now, what would it be?

Think about this ...

Of Death
and Worry

In life, there are only two things to worry about:
you are well or you are sick.

If you are well, there is nothing to worry about.

If you are sick, there are only two things to worry about:
you will get well or you will die.

If you get well, there is nothing to worry about.

If you die, there are only two things to worry about:
you will go to heaven or hell.

If you go to heaven, there is nothing to worry about.

If you go to hell, you'll be so busy shaking hands with
all your friends
you'll have no time to worry.

MESSAGE 19
CHOICE

Decide your own future

Life presents you with many opportunities and with many choices. There comes a time in your life when you must decide between where you are and where you want to be. The choices you make can either make or break you. You will have to live with your decisions until you make further changes.

It is never too late to become what you really want to be provided you are prepared to pay the price associated with the change. The choice is yours.

Are you going to be an optimist or a pessimist into the future? It's your choice. What you believe about yourself determines how people treat you.

Hindsight is valuable only if you take the lessons from your mistakes and missed opportunities

Q With the benefit of hindsight, would you have made different choices in your life/ business? Which ones in particular would you have changed? What one step could you take today that would kick-start your new you?

MESSAGE 20

VISION

Imagine the future – live with purpose

Albert Einstein, winner of the Nobel Prize for physics and one of the most influential people of the 20th and 21st centuries, said: 'Imagination is more important than knowledge. For knowledge is limited to all we now know and understand, while imagination embraces the entire world and all there ever will be to know and understand.'

If you want to improve your skills, your standard of living, your quality of life, your business, your degree of happiness, imagine it as though it is already happening. Use your imagination to create a vision of your perfect world. Imagine great health and financial freedom. There may be a price in the

Imagination is intelligence having fun. Everything of importance has been said before by somebody who did not discover it

short-term to get there long term. Are you prepared to pay the price?

Anais Nis said, 'You see things as you are, not as they are in reality'. Life is a series of present moments which you can manage to your advantage. Set your ideals high enough to inspire you and low enough to encourage you. Where you have come from can't be changed. Perhaps, right now, you want to change your destination.

Your vision launches your intention. To realize your vision, fuel it by purpose and by passion and follow it by action. Decide right now and plan the next phase of your life journey.

What pictures have you in your mind about your future? Focus on those pictures and you will enhance the possibility of them becoming real. Draw your dreams on a napkin or a sheet of paper. Then draw them better on another napkin or sheet of paper. Leave them for a day or so and draw them again. You may find that you have changed your mind. Keep at it. Revise them, change them, adapt them and develop them. Then try to write actions that would make them happen.

Most new products are not new inventions but rather rediscoveries of existing products with imagination

Only those who dare to fail greatly can ever achieve greatly

Robert F. Kennedy

We don't like their sound, and guitar music is on the way out

Decca Recording Company rejecting the Beatles, 1962

Vision is the art of seeing things invisible

Jonathan Swift

A good idea is delicate. It can be killed by a sneer. It can be stabbed to death by a joke or worried to death by a frown. You must not be afraid to fail over and over again. It is essential to creativity. If people never did silly things, nothing intelligent would ever get done.

No one can possibly achieve any real and lasting success by being a conformist. If you only look at what is, you might never attain what could be. Yesterday is not ours to recover but tomorrow is ours to manage. The future belongs to those who prepare for it today. It comes one day at a time.

If you are part of the herd, you cannot go any further than the herd. It's always too late by the time the herd arrives. Wishing for something to happen is just that. Act to make it happen.

There are many examples of missed opportunities. In reality we could draw up our own list of missed opportunities. Opportunities are more transparent in hindsight than in foresight. That's why it's so important to challenge our minds to understand that there are always

So we went to Atari and said, "We've got this amazing thing, even built with some of your parts and what do you think about funding us? Or we'll give it to you. We just want to do it. Pay our salary – we'll come work for you.' They said, "No". Then we went to Hewlett-Packard who said, "We don't need you. You haven't got through college yet"

Steve Jobs, Apple Computers

Q What are you passionate about?

better solutions and more opportunities on the way.

Exposing yourself to reading, travelling and education programmes is important as you will enhance the possibility that you will spot something of interest and of value that you can apply to your life, your systems or processes.

I am challenging you here to live your life with purpose. If you don't know where you are going, any road will do, hence the necessity for clarity of purpose as expressed in your mission statement. Don't wait around for permission. Do it and, if necessary, apologize for your actions after. If it's worth achieving, it's worth paying the price.

Q Influences, thoughts, feelings, beliefs, action, inputs and output can be different lodgements in the Bank of Life. Can they eventually lead to an invoice?

What the human mind can conceive and believe, it can accomplish

What is now proved was once only imagined

William Blake

This "telephone" has too many shortcomings to be seriously considered as a means of communication. The device is inherently of no value to us

Western Union memo, 1876

Think about this ...

Plant Your Garden Today

First, plant 3 rows of peas:
Patience
Promptness
Prayer

Next, plant 3 rows of squash:
Squash gossip
Squash indifference
Squash criticism

Then, plant 3 rows of lettuce:
Let us be loyal
Let us be true to our obligations
Let us be unselfish

Finish, with 4 rows of turnip:
Turn up when needed
Turn up with a smile
Turn up with a vision
Turn up with determination

MESSAGE 21

LEADERSHIP

Create the future

Peter Drucker, the business management expert, explained the difference between a manager and a leader. He said: 'A good manager manages a business at the present; a great leader manages the business into the future.'

Leadership is about achieving results through others. It's not necessarily related to experience, formal education or any of the other things that so many claim is leadership. It's consistent delivery of results and recovery from failures. Leaders regard failures as stepping stones to get them over the 'valley of death' between creation of ideas and bringing those ideas to reality in the future. They learn from each mistake.

Confront the barriers of conditioning

Our chief want is someone who will inspire us to be what we know we could be

Ralph Waldo Emerson

Good leaders know when to listen and let others do the talking

Leaders tend to focus externally. They survey the environment for opportunities and threats. This informs their vision. They communicate their vision to those on their team or staff members or troops on the ground in a clear and meaningful way. The quality of leadership is reflected in the quality of the followers.

Captain Robert Scott and Sir Ernest Shackleton, leaders of the most extreme expeditions for science to the desolate landscape of the Antarctic required the ultimate in human endurance. Tom Crean from Annascaul, Co. Kerry, one of their forty-member team of 1901 was acknowledged for his abilities when King George presented the Albert Medal to him at Buckingham Palace in 1913. He had on his own initiative and at risk to his life walked 35 miles across the ice of the South Pole to save his team members. He had been sought for several expeditions to help his leaders

> Do not be afraid of going slowly; be afraid only of standing still
>
> *I've got to follow them; I am their leader*
>
> Ledru-Rollin

Q If I phoned you, would you become the leader of a group of people wanting to climb a mountain?

Leaders are the architects; managers are the builders

John Mariotti

He who follows the crowd will usually get no further than the crowd

Get results through others

realize their dreams. In his own space, he, too, was a leader.

A core task of a leader is to create and transfer a sense of direction and urgency for team members so that they will commit to the vision and make whatever individual and team changes are needed to make that vision become real. Leaders say: 'It's not what you get from the experience that counts, but what you become by it.'

Leadership is the ability to translate vision into reality. All things are created in the mind before they are delivered on the ground. Leadership is not a position; it's a choice and a skill. It is not about creating blind enthusiasm for some abstract objective. It's about influencing others to march in a particular direction.

Rather than launching into the unknown, the task of leadership is to make the status quo more skilful and more equipped for the adventure. Managers do things right, leaders do the right thing. Leaders lead people and manage tangible assets.

Good leaders surround themselves with people who are better than themselves in necessary areas. They work smart by utilizing everyone's potential. Leaders follow their passion rather than their pension. If you are a leader, don't continue to postpone your living until you are ready. Some leaders have high spikes and low lows. Many suffer from bouts of depression because things are not happening fast enough for them.

Leaders have a continuum of decision-making styles ranging from autocratic type to the complete consultative type. Leaders can be either people-focussed or task-focussed. People-orientated leaders are best in non-competitive type environments. Task-orientated leaders are best in competitive environments, where quick, tangible results are critical.

Enthusiasm reflects confidence, spreads good cheer, raises morale, inspires associates, arouses loyalty, and laughs at adversity... it is beyond price

Allan Cox

Leaders make goals of their dreams, rather than dream about their goals

A good leader takes a little more than his share of the blame, a little less than his share of the credit

Arnold Glasow

Think about this ...

How high can you jump?

Flea trainers have observed a predictable and strange habit of fleas. They are trained by putting them in a cardboard box with a top on it. The fleas will jump up and hit the top of the cardboard box over and over and over again. As you watch them jump and hit the lid, something very interesting becomes obvious. The fleas continue to jump, but they are no longer jumping high enough to hit the top.

When you take off the lid, the fleas will continue to jump, but they will not jump out of the box. They won't jump out because they can't jump out. Why? The reason is simple. They have conditioned themselves to jump just so high. Once they have conditioned themselves to jump just so high, that's all they can do!

Many times, people do the same thing. They restrict themselves and never reach their potential. Just like the fleas, they fail to jump higher, thinking they are doing all they can do. Many of us are too conditioned by the negativity out there and dance to the recurring tune: "You can't; you're no good."

Roger Bannister didn't just break the four-minute mile record. He broke the psychological barrier. This opened the gap for many to follow in quick succession.

When we change our beliefs, great achievement is possible.

MESSAGE 22
IMPACT

Empower others

Treat others as you'd like to be treated. To accomplish great things, you'll be limited and constrained if you act alone. You'll need people. Influencing is a necessary skill which we must constantly strive to perfect in a team. None of us is an island and we need to influence the necessary people so that our vision can be energised.

At critical points, we are more vulnerable to be influenced by others for good or for bad. At these vulnerable points, even small external interventions can have huge impacts.

Compassion can cure more sins than condemnation. Respect everyone. I know of managers who have trampled on staff members. Over time, former employees took ownership of business and fired those same managers who in the past had bullied them. People influence each other to reach their goals.

At home, in work, at school, you are always influencing people. In business you are always

> Empower people and you will be empowered
>
> *I bring you the gift of these four words: 'I believe in you'*
>
> *Blaise Pascal*

influencing customers in some way, strongly or weakly, positively or negatively, intentionally or unintentionally. When you control your words and actions to produce a desired response, you possess one of the most useful skills anyone can have.

Many tactics are used in marketing and promotions to influence customers to buy or to remind or to maintain their loyalty. One of these tactics is the use of creative design to convey the messages with impact. Wording, meaning, sound, tone of voice, shape, size, colour, brand image, reputation, the attitudes of staff members are vital elements of the messages used to get prospects and customers to purchase products and services and to maintain their custom.

The use or misuse of language is a major influencer. If you don't want to do something, be positive and say 'No'. Don't apologise. This is about you positively taking charge of you. The degree to which you have self-control the more positive will be your influence.

Your language is the outward verbalization of your inner beliefs. It is a reflection of the way your mind works and it will be a major influencer on your audience. Your audience sees, hears and notes everything. They will interpret it and they will be influenced by it.

Q Name one person in your circle of family, neighbours or friends you can empower with a word of praise or a call to action today

Think about this ...

Criticism

If an impulse comes to say

Some unthoughtful word today

That may drive a friend away,

Don't say it!

Professional management

Empowering people and building business

MESSAGE 23
COMMUNICATION

Send, receive and feedback

The latest news. The best teapot in the world. The best solution to war or disease. The best solution to money problems. You will have no effect, no impact with your ideas or your solutions unless you share them with people. That sharing comes through active communication.

To communicate your new idea, product or service to your partners, business prospects or potential customers you will need a communications plan. This may be as simple as creating a database of people to whom to send your message or invitation. You may create a flyer and a letter and send it to your database of contacts. You may place messages on social media, or advertisements on newspapers, magazines, radio or television.

Communication is a two-way street. There is the giver and the receiver. Often the receiver internalises a completely different message from what was intended by the giver

He knows most who says he knows least

Confucius

If it's an idea for a new product or a concept for a new service that you believe is going to make you a fortune be sure to protect your intellectual property (I.P.).

The word communication comes from the Latin *communico*, meaning share. A communication model has elements of sender and receiver. The sender sends the carefully constructed message; the receiver receives it and decodes it and decides to act on it or not.

The key to keeping the communication alive and going is feedback. That is the ultimate sharing. It closes one loop and starts the next loop of communication. The acid test of your communication effectiveness is your ability to influence what others are saying about you and your business.

It is wiser to choose what you say than say what you choose. There are some things one can't or shouldn't tell but once told, they cannot be untold

It is the province of knowledge to speak, and it is the privilege of wisdom to listen

Oliver Wendell Holmes, Jr.

Q What truth can you tell someone today to improve their life?

Think about this ...

Communication Difficulties

Complaints to a local government department:

"Will you please send someone to mend the garden path? My wife tripped and fell on it yesterday and now she is pregnant."

"Can you please tell me when the repairs will be done as my wife is about to become an expectant mother?"

"The toilet is blocked and we cannot bath the children until it is cleared."

"Will you please send a man to look at my water; it is a funny colour and not fit to drink."

"Our lavatory seat is broken in half and now it is in three pieces."

"Our kitchen floor is damp. We have two children and would like a third so will you please send someone around to do something about it."

"I've got arthritis and heart failure in both feet and knees".

"I am unable to walk now as my dog has died".

"I hope you will send your driver as my husband is quite useless".

"I cannot walk up a hill unless it is down and the hill to your clinic is up".

MESSAGE 24

CHANGE

Manage change or it will manage you

You are currently where you are, based to a great extent on the decisions you made in the past. If you are satisfied with your present conditions, stay as you are. If you want a better future, make some changes.

Dr. Spencer Johnson in his inspirational world best-seller *Who Moved my Cheese* says: "Be ready to change quickly and enjoy it again and again as they keep moving the cheese." The cheese is his metaphor for what we want to have in life.

Change comes about in most people's lives by chance, by crisis or by choice. Chance and Crisis favours those who are prepared for them. If you have Choice, you can more easily plan your move to a better place.

Mistakes are signposts to success. Opportunity comes gift-wrapped in problems

You must be the change you wish to see in the world

Mahatma Gandhi

Change is happening every minute, every hour, every day, every month and every year. Nothing stays the same. Change is happening all the time. People, the weather, the seasons, the economy, the markets, politics are forever changing.

You may not notice change. It is amazing how so much seems to be moving along so smoothly. One day you are hit by a major change or by a series of major changes which come all at the same time to create 'the perfect storm'. What can you do? Do nothing? Just do your best? Muddle through? Or you can anticipate the next major change, prepare for it, become adaptable to change and when it comes, manage it. Change is inevitable in your life. Do you want to manage it in your favour?

Are you suffering enough right now to want to change? Or would you prefer to wait until you feel worse? Are you half-hearted about your business or career? Are you a creature of habit, repeating an old formula but doing it faster and sweating more?

If your answer is "Yes" to any of these questions, consider starting a change

All mankind is divided into three classes: those that are immovable, those that are movable, and those that move

Benjamin Franklin

Life is controlled by the law of cause and effect. Thoughts are the cause. Changed behaviour is the effect. To achieve the effect, control your thoughts

process so that you can become what you are capable of becoming.

Travel, reading, training programmes and seminars open up your mind to what change is possible. Get excited and get eager to get out of your comfort zone. You are today where your thoughts of yesterday have brought you. Guilt about times gone by and what you might have done had you known will waste your energy. Use the time that you now have. Tomorrow you will be where your thoughts of today take you. Operating as before just leads to more of the same.

There is no point in waiting for what you'd love to do. Change causes stress but you can manage this stress to achieve your goal.

Everything in life has a price. There is a price for doing and a price for not doing. Win the debate in your own head about the price you are prepared to pay.

Change is a process. It is natural that you resist change. What you know is less threatening than what you don't know. Change also holds the keys to your future success. The only way you can liberate yourself from the conditioning of your life journey is by taking responsibility for your choices. Don't be afraid to take a bigger step and change.

When I am wrong, dear Lord, make me easy to change and when I am right, make me easy to live with

Peter Marshall

Q What small change could you make and what small victory could you have today?

Think about this ...

What to do when you are
riding a
dead horse

What do you do when you discover that you are riding a dead horse? Instead of buying a stronger whip, changing riders, scolding horse and rider, re-structuring the dead horse's reward scale to contain a performance-related element, making the dead horse work late shifts and weekends, appointing a committee to study the horse, arranging to visit to other countries to see how other cultures ride horses, lowering the standards so that dead horses can be included, hiring outside contractors to ride the dead horse, harnessing several dead horses together to increase speed, doing a productivity study to see if lighter riders would improve the dead horse's performance, declaring that as the dead horse does not have to be fed, it is less costly, carries lower overheads and therefore contributes substantially more to the bottom line of the economy than do some other horses, rewriting the expected performance requirements for all horses and the highly effective tactic of promoting the dead horse to a supervisory position, after all of that, your best tactic is probably to dismount.

You probably know of organisations or groups with similar horses.

Where is the
dead horse
in your patch?

MESSAGE 25
INFLUENCE

Give good example

When Bob Geldof and Midge Ure of Band Aid were organising their Live Aid concert transmitted across the world in 1985, to raise funds to alleviate hunger in Africa, they used the influence of every friend and contact to achieve their goal. Live Aid united world famous singers and musicians in a cause that made a difference.

Parents, siblings, teachers, neighbours, friends, work colleagues, community leaders, business leaders, politicians and pop-stars are influencers. The role you play, the work you do, what you own, what others think of you and what you think others think of you are influencers.

The work or profession you do puts a label on you regarding your job or vocation. What you have involves all the "stuff" you have accumulated such as your house, your car and your partner. What others think of you can be a major barrier

If you can't convince them, confuse them

A politician's tactic

Nothing hurts us like the things we don't say to help influence other people to our advantage

preventing you from reaching your dream. Everything in life is relative and no matter how much you accumulate you will perceive someone else to have more.

No matter in what phase of your life you are now, there are always people ahead of you and behind you.

Influencing is about moving things forward without pushing, forcing or telling others what to do. It's about encouraging people to join you in your mission and exciting them to make a big contribution of their time and support. Change is best achieved through influence rather than through imposition.

According to the Law of Reflection, the world reflects back to you on the basis of how you present yourself to it. If you smile, the world will smile back at you. However, if you are too anxious to be liked and get approval you are driving your life's motor car forward looking out through the rear view mirror instead of looking through the front windscreen.

Trust is critical for influence. Building trust is equivalent to building your brand. A brand is only as strong as the targeted customer's degree of positive or negative response to it. Trust is hard won and easily lost. Trust tends to run parallel with your confidence and that of your customer.

Every human interaction involves a complex process of persuasion and influence. You have two choices: either to be influenced or to influence. You can persuade others to help you or you can be persuaded to help them. It is mostly one or the other.

Ask for what you want from those who have the capacity to say "Yes".

This is a powerful tactic and is so much more efficient than a lot of the shadow boxing that goes on. Give appreciation from your heart. Our deepest urge is to be important and appreciated. The desire to be important and feel appreciated has driven all great achievements.

We all have degrees of influence. Stephen Covey, the world-renowned management author, represents these degrees of influence by three circles. The inner circle is the Circle of Control where you have control over the variables. Use your management skills in this circle. Next is the Circle of Influence. You may not have full control over what happens in this circle but you may influence some things in your favour. The outer circle is the Circle of Concern. You may have no control but to gain competitive advantage focus on how you are going to strategically position yourself.

You are always influencing people in some way. Control your words and actions to give good example.

As we go through life's journey we are influenced by both people and events but in turn, we, too, are influencers on others. This carries responsibilities.

> *I really loved her and I nearly told her once*
>
> *A variation of Ireland's chart-topping song, 'I Useta Lover' by The Saw Doctors*

> Pull the string, and it will follow wherever you wish. Push it, and it will go nowhere at all
>
> *Dwight D. Eisenhower*

MESSAGE 26
BUSINESS

Think win, win, win

John Harvey Jones, once chairman of ICI and presenter of the BBC programme, *Trouble-shooter*, said: 'Business leadership is demanding of time, concentration, sheer grinding brain power and the ability to live an intrinsically unhealthy existence with some sort of control. The hours are, of necessity, very long, and one's body is continuously exposed to cruel punishment, not of the sort that toughens the muscles and develops strength but rather of the sort that just places demands without producing the ability to cope with them.'

That's business leadership as most business people know it. Business consumes every waking minute and if you are a business leader it demands all the talents, physical, emotional and psychological resources that you can give to make it succeed. And at the

Under capitalism, man exploits man; under communism, it's just the opposite

A friendship founded on business is better than a business founded on friendship

Treat your customer as an appreciating asset

end, through no fault of your own, you may fail. If you are to live and succeed better, get up again and drive on.

Business people are entrepreneurs. Entrepreneurialism is a characteristic identified by Richard Cantillon, a native of Ballyheigue, Co. Kerry, father of modern economics and originator of the concept of 'opportunity cost'. In his manuscript *Essai Sur La Nature Du Commerce En General* (1730), he applied his concepts to describe those who get things done, use the scarcest of resources, take risks and speculate on opportunities.

Richard Branson of Virgin said that he survived in business through making mistakes. He said that the more mistakes you make, the more you should learn.

Business provides the life-blood of the nation keeping people employed, taxes paid, bureaucracies alive, governments in office and attempts to provide a good future and a quality lifestyle for every citizen.

Customers are appreciating assets. In the end, all business operations can be reduced to four words: customers, staff, product, profit. A business person will develop clear

The longer you go on without being exposed to an event such as the recession, the more vulnerable you will be to it

A business is like an automobile – it has to be driven to get results

Don't worry because a rival imitates you. As long as he follows in your tracks, he can't pass you

There is nothing more requisite in business than despatch

Joseph Addison

strategies for each of these four "pillars" of business. Good customers are the first pillar.

Your business must from this day forward live in the future which is as yet unborn. Make some assumptions about the future trends so that you can make decisions about where you are going to put your investments. Predicting with consistent accuracy is difficult since most plans are just predictions.

Long-range planning deals with the future of present decisions. The macro economy keeps changing and if you want to win, you too must keep pace with it. There is little correlation between business success and hard work. Being street-wise and being able to navigate your way through the various roadblocks is more important than hard work. Profit comes not from the end job but from the idea behind it. Become the ideas generator and let others deliver.

Successful business people have a high need to achieve success. They achieve their objectives through the commitment of people. Think Win! Win! Win! Win for your customer, win for the business and staff and win for you.

The best preparation for good work tomorrow is to do good work today

Elbert Hubbard

We always plan too much and always think too little

Joseph Schumpeter

To predict the future we need logic but we also need faith and imagination, which can sometimes defy logic itself

Arthur C. Clarke

Q What are you invoicing in your business?

MESSAGE 27
ECONOMICS

Expect cycles and shocks

Milton Friedman, the celebrated Nobel-prizewinning authority on economics, said that if people can learn more about the way the world works they can contribute to forming a public opinion which will be in favour of things that will help society instead of hurt it.

Economists are historians, not clairvoyants

You have €100 to spend. Do you put it in a safe and hope that over time, its value will increase? Do you give it all to people who are less well off than you? Do you give some of it to rich friends to make them richer or to less well-off people to make them richer? Do you keep some for the rainy day and spend the rest? Do you add value by using some of the money to build a career or a business?

The fundamental principle of economics is that all resources – land, labour, capital and entrepreneurialism – are scarce. How those

Q How are you positioning yourself to take advantage of the emerging cycle?

resources are used or deployed depends on choices made by decision-makers in your county, in Dublin, in Brussels, in Frankfurt, Wall Street, Washington, Beijing, Hong Kong and every other country in the world. Everything is interconnected. A rumour in Wexford can have an impact on Dublin and on London.

You can influence those decisions and policy changes to your own benefit and to the benefit of your own community by continuously questioning government and local authority policies and by raising the issues with your friends, neighbours, politicians and government department decision-makers.

What influences your own choices? What influences the decisions made by government? What resources have been squandered in the past? What resources have been plundered from our future? A prudent decision-maker might consider how those scarce resources would be used better to provide sustainable security for five years from now.

The decisions by families, by governments, by businesses, and by the economists who advise them on the use of scarce resources are vital to the future of everybody in society. The herd instinct and group-think overwhelms rational

We have government of the people by the bureaucracy for the bureaucracy

Milton Friedman, Ph.D.

God created weather forecasters in order to make economists look good

thought. Whole governments and politicians override good economics for political expediency – to get re-elected or to cause some change that they think is better than that advised.

The economics environment is like the seasons of the year. It comes in cycles. You may expect spring, summer and autumn to be followed by winter. Every so often you'll have thunder and lightning and torrential rain or heavy snow. Whole countries have periods of economic calm and prosperity. Inevitably, these will be followed by periods of extreme ups and downs, shocks, crashes, recessions and depressions.

The controls being implemented for the current economic cycle are usually designed for the dynamics of the past economic cycle. The next cycle will have its own dynamics. Controls always follow the event, not precede them. Instead of following the herd, you can be a contrarian. Have you made some provision for future shocks?

Q Are you bothered enough by the emerging opportunities to make the decision to pay the price? There is a price for doing and a price for not doing.

MANAGEMENT

Manage the variables you have control over

Take control. Whether managing your home, your work life, your personal life and career or your businesses, manage only what you have control over. Don't waste your scarce resources of time, energy, money and opportunity trying to manage things that are far too big for you and over which you have no control. That's one of the big secrets of successful management.

Chief executives of major corporations employing perhaps thousands of people try to manage, at most, only five people. Those five are usually their management team. It would be humanly impossible for a chief executive to manage more than his or her management team.

Focus on solutions, not faults

Never mind who you praise but be careful who you blame

The worker who is denied the opportunity of making decisions begins to regard as important the decisions he is allowed to take. He becomes fussy about filing and form filling

That is why chief executives apply remote control over hundreds and thousands of employees and suppliers and agents through their management teams.

In your personal or home life, try to not take on more than you can manage with a stretch and have control over. There will be times in your life when you will be unable to control the many things that are going on around you. If things get beyond your personal control, engage remote control and delegate work and responsibilities to others whom you trust and are answerable to you.

Use the '4 Ds' of management – Do it, Dump it or Delay it until you find a solution or Delegate to others to do it for you. Surround yourself with the best people you can find. Delegate responsibility and parallel authority and then don't interfere. Never tell people how to do things. Agree with them what you want them to achieve and they will surprise you. Delegate to the lowest possible level, manage by exception and inspect what you expect. Be clear about what you expect in the measurable outputs and the areas of responsibility. Be careful that you don't take back the job

I praise loudly. I blame softly

Catherine the Great, 1729-1796

The only thing that saves us from bureaucracy is its inefficiency

The higher my rank, the more humbly I behave. The greater my power, the less I exercise it. The richer my wealth, the more I give away. Thus I avoid, respectively, envy and spite and misery

Sun Shu Ao, Chinese minister, 600BC

which you previously delegated. Give people the authority and the responsibility to deliver an agreed output.

We grow only if we stretch ourselves against the relevant best and develop a plan to beat this best. A manager is not one who can do the work better than his people; a manager gets people to do the work better than he or she can. Good managers never put off until tomorrow what they can manage today.

Never tell people how to do things. Tell them what to do and they will surprise you with their ingenuity

General George S. Patton Jr

If you see a company where the ego rules the brain you'd better sell the shares

No man will work for your interests unless they are his

David Seabury

Q What small task or challenge can you kill off today?

Think about this ...

Four Steps to Achievement

Plan purposefully

Prepare prayerfully

Proceed positively

Pursue persistently.

MESSAGE 29
STRATEGY

Think how

Sun Tzu, the Chinese military general who wrote *The Art of War* more than 2000 years ago, is said by many to be the father of strategy. The essence of what he says is: Know your strategy before you act. You may have tactics, but without strategy, you will lose.

Every day John's dad would play with him after coming home from work. John looked forward to these precious moments. One night in order to keep John busy while he needed to do some other work, his dad took a map of the world and cut it into small irregular shaped pieces like a jigsaw and told John to try and put the map together piece by piece.

About half an hour later John came back to his dad and said he was finished. His dad was surprised, saying, 'That's impossible.

Use available data and common sense to make better assumptions about the evolving trends

The reasonable man adapts himself to the world. The unreasonable one persists in trying to adapt the world to himself; therefore all progress depends on unreasonable men

George Bernard Shaw

Let's go see.' And sure enough, there was the picture of the world; all put together, every piece in its place. His dad said, 'That's amazing! How did you do that?' John said, 'It was simple. On the back of the page was a picture of a man. When I put the man together the whole world fell into place!'

John had a challenge. He studied the problem. He created a strategy. He found a solution.

Your strategy comprises your vision and your goals and a roadmap. On a sheet of paper, write out your dream of where you want to be in three years' time. Research thoroughly the steps, the time, the money, the resources that you need to get there. Then write out the steps that you are going to take. Cost it and monitor your progress. You may need lots of time and advice to achieve this but it will be worth it. It will be less costly than finding out by mistake.

In strategy it is important to see distant things as if they were close and to take a distant view of close things.

We often get in quicker by the back door than by the front

Men never plan to be failures; they simply fail to plan to be successful

William A. Ward

Be careful when others are greedy and be greedy when others are fearful

Warren Buffett

Entrepreneurs think strategically. They leave the detail to others. They tend to be right-brained. They are always looking "outside the box" for a smarter opportunity and the means of achieving it. They see new patterns and make connections. They drive along the trail to the mountain and leave a few signposts here and there for others to follow. They expect those who follow them to leave more signposts for their followers.

If you want a different output into the future, make a different input. It is foolish to continue to do the exact same thing and expect to get a different result

Work in this order: Think – Plan – Act – Measure – Celebrate

When the river is murky, be patient and let the waters flow to clear the mud

The way to get started is to quit talking and get doing

Imagination can change a problem and turn it into a goldmine

Planning without action is futile; action without planning is fatal

I cannot give you a formula for success but I can give you the formula for failure – which is: Try to please everybody

Herbert Bayard Swope

MESSAGE 30
TACTICS

Complete one step at a time

n football, players learn and internalise myriad tactics to be used in different situations that they encounter on the field of play. In the game of chess, players use several tactics or moves on the chess board to outwit their opponents.

In business, managers set goals to achieve sales targets and write a strategy followed by setting tactics of advertising, promotions, publicity, sponsorships and social media activities in order to get customers and keep them. In the home, parents set goals for themselves and for their children to achieve education, get a job, set up a business, gain independence, self-sufficiency and financial freedom.

Your goal might be to buy a car. Your strategy might be to use savings and borrowings to do so. Your tactics might

Business is simple. You ask people to sell something to you at one price. You do something with it to add to its value and then ask them to buy from you at a different price. Your profit is the difference, less your operating costs

Ask for help. You won't make it in life on your own

be to visit several car showrooms to get the best possible deal, go to a bank or financial institution to get the best possible terms of finance and repay any money borrowed and sell or exchange your old car.

Tactics are the big and small steps that you build into your strategy to reach your goals. Achievers in sport and games and business management use tactics every day as the major part of their strategy to achieve their goals.

If your goals, strategy and tactics are built into a master system that you follow over a period of time, the system will automatically take over your effort to achieve whatever you want to achieve. It'll become part of your subconscious. Managers use the term 'systemization' to describe this process.

Start by visualising where you want to be in three years' time. The result of your mind-storm will be your goals or objectives. Research the options and possibilities necessary to devise a strategy to achieve your goals or objectives within that timeframe. When you have set the

Asking is the world's most powerful but neglected secret to success and happiness. Become smart at using Kipling's six honest serving men: Who? What? Where? When?, Why? and How?

Don't be beaten by rejections. Keep asking until you get a "YES"

Don't burn any bridges. You might want to travel back over that valley

strategy, research and set the tactics or steps necessary to achieve your goals. Complete each step, one at a time.

Know what you really want. I can't help you if I don't know what you want. It's up to you to ask for specific help. A fuzzy request gives the potential giver an opportunity to avoid giving you what you need. Don't be afraid to think big. You may not have the opportunity of going back for a second bite. You can modify your strategy based on your constraints.

Who has the capacity and the motivation to help you? It's not smart to approach someone for help if they don't have the capacity to help you. If you don't have positional power over the potential giver, use influence. Can you use someone who out-ranks your target-giver to open the door for you?

What's in it for the potential giver? Understand their motivational "hot buttons" and then play to their agenda. While you may not be able to deliver tangible benefits to your

If you ask in the appropriate way, you can have what you desire. Set your goals and ask people for specific help to get you there

Ask with a smile and be silent. The person who breaks this silence tends to lose

Live up to your obligations and promises. Asking for something carries obligations

potential giver, you can focus on giving them intangible benefits, such as making them feel important and appreciated. You will have to give a little in order to receive a lot.

Perfect your asking technique. Try to be smarter at knowing 'How' to ask your potential giver. Show them respect and courtesy. But never beg. Use the tactic of requesting rather than demanding. This gives the target the opportunity to say "YES" or "NO". They won't feel trapped. Demanding will encourage them to become defensive with a probable negative result for you.

Try to get to "We" as soon as possible

Asking and giving go together. The more you give, the more you get back. This is the Law of Reflection. If you don't ask for what you want, you probably won't get it. Asking can make big things happen for you

Q What is the first small step you will take this week to kick-start your process of asking?

Think about this ...

Just for today

Just for today, I will try to live through this day only, and not tackle my whole life problem at once. I can do something for twelve hours that would appal me if I felt that I had to keep it up for a lifetime.

Just for today, I will be happy. This assumes to be true what Abraham Lincoln said, that "most folks are as happy as they make up their minds to be."

Just for today, I will try to strengthen my mind. I will study. I will learn something useful. I will not be a mental loafer. I will read something that requires effort, thought and concentration.

Just for today, I will adjust myself to what is, and not try to adjust everything to my own desires. I will take my "luck" as it comes, and fit myself to it.

Just for today, I will exercise my soul in three ways: I will do somebody a good turn, and not get found out. I will do at least two things I don't want to – just

for exercise. I will not show anyone that my feelings are hurt; they may be hurt, but today I will not show it.

Just for today, I will be agreeable. I will look as well as I can, dress becomingly, talk low, act courteously, criticize not one bit, not find fault with anything and not try to improve or regulate anybody except myself.

Just for today, I will have a programme. I may not follow it exactly, but I will have it. I will save myself from two pests: hurry and indecision.

Just for today, I will have a quiet half hour all by myself, and relax. During this half hour, sometime, I will try to get a better perspective of my life.

Just for today, I will be unafraid. Especially I will not be afraid to enjoy what is beautiful, and to believe that as I give to the world, so the world will give to me.

– *Anon*

MESSAGE 31
POWER

Do good with your own resources

A farmer I knew had six sheepdogs which he fed at the same time every day giving each one an equally filled bowl of the best dog-food. The dogs would whine and bark until he fed them. If he was a minute late with the daily ration, the dogs would whine and bark and growl until he filled their bowls. When the bowls were empty, all the dogs, except one, would walk quietly away, satisfied. That lone dog was never satisfied although he got exactly the same amount as that allocated to his fellow dogs. He would howl for more. The farmer would succumb to the dog's plea. In order to quell the dog's barking he would give him an extra portion. The moral of the story is profound – the dog who barks most gets more. The dog used the power of his bark. He got what he wanted.

Power tends to corrupt and absolute power corrupts absolutely

Reputation is an idle and most false imposition, oft got without merit and lost without deserving

Iago in 'Othello' by William Shakespeare

Everyone has power. Power to accept. Power to refuse. Power to influence. Power to change. Power to manipulate or coerce or secure compliance of others. Power to do great good. You may have power beyond your imagination.

Most people use their position power to achieve outcomes of benefit to themselves, their families and their communities and businesses. The use and abuse of position power by people to achieve outcomes that they desire, is the subject of numerous debates, theses and theories.

If a baby cries, the baby will have power until its need or want is satisfied. In a business, the manager may have power to hire, penalize and fire. In a democracy, people may exercise their power to elect one candidate to a position of power and punish another. In a dictatorship, the dictator may have power over the lives of the people.

You may have power but you may not have influence. You may have authority

Adversarial power relationships work only if you never have to see or work with your antagonists again

The greatest power is often simple patience

E. Joseph Cossman

The great tend eventually to become bad

but you may not have power. You may have influence, but you may not have authority or power. Supporters of a hurling team have influence. However, the team manager has ultimate power and the team members have a lesser power but much more power than those who are not in the game.

How to use the power that you have is often constrained by circumstances outside of your control. Society can exercise a coercive power over people. Rules and regulations of bureaucracies can limit your power. The power that you have can move mountains. To use it responsibly, your challenge is to do good.

All power is built on trust. When you make people dependent on your agenda, you will continue to have a hold over them. In order to get going, you need ability followed by reputation. Later, the sequence changes to reputation followed by ability. Your reputation is equivalent to your brand name. Keep promoting it in your relevant market niches to retain your power. Unused power slips imperceptibly into the hands of another.

The formula to enhance your power position is to build on two pillars: no. 1. Make others dependent on you and no. 2. Reduce your dependence on others. Can you use this formula to your advantage?

Q: How can you increase your relative power position? What will you do with it?

MESSAGE 32

THE PARETO PRINCIPLE

Focus on the productive 20%

Vilfredo Pareto, an Italian economist who lived from 1848 to 1923, developed the concept of the 80/20 principle. It is often referred to as 'the 80/20 rule' or the Pareto Principle or the Pareto Law. This rule can be applied to home life and living, sport, business, sales, marketing and many other aspects of life and business. It means that eighty per cent of everything is wasted or abused or less effective and that focus on the twenty per cent of most things will be effective, profitable or beneficial.

Eighty per cent of time is wasted while twenty per cent is productive. Twenty per cent of sales people generate eighty per cent of revenue. Eighty per cent of work is done within twenty per cent of the time allowed.

The Pareto Law is also known as The Principle of Least Effort. In practice this means that a minority of your effort can lead to the majority of output. Stop thinking 'Average'. Start thinking '80/20'.

Good managers use the concept when they ask for the greatest output from the smallest input. Examine your sales performance and see how near your performance is to the 80/20 rule. The high performers create wealth, and at the same time, low performers leak it.

You can achieve more with less by focusing on the twenty per cent that works for you. Find the twenty per cent 'sweet spot'. Most of what we really achieve occurs during a very small proportion of our working life. Identify and optimise this critical twenty per cent. The key is not effort, but finding the right thing to achieve. Those who think first and then act are more likely to succeed than those who act first and then think. Think 80/20 and eventually you will start acting by this principle and gaining corresponding results.

If you want to become a successful business manager, apply the 80/20 rule to your strategic thinking. Use it to identify where you are making money, which customers to drop and which market segments to develop. This will allow you to concentrate your resources and win.

As you go through life, how much of your time are you engaged in really satisfying work? Can you reposition yourself so that you become the top performer in your niche? The top twenty per cent of performers take eighty per cent of the goodies. The few have most. Winners take nearly all.

Focus eighty per cent of your marketing budget on the twenty per cent of the niche that's capable of generating eighty per cent of your revenue. Leverage more from this critical twenty per cent than from the non-performing eighty per cent. The market is pragmatic and pays you for your output only. It doesn't care how busy you are.

By delisting marginal products and customers, you will boost your net profits.

Everyone has some degree of an investment portfolio. That investment may not be just in monetary terms. It may be in a big personal investment in your career. Now that you have made this investment, use the 80/20 rule to get a smarter return on your investment of time, money and your other resources to achieve it.

To achieve satisfaction and happiness in your personal life, apply the 80/20 rule. Identify the people, situations and events that give you most happiness and satisfaction. Identify the eighty per cent who clutter your life, use you, rob you of energy, and engage in waffle that gives you least satisfaction. Gradually starve them of attention and oxygen. Give your preferred twenty per cent more oxygen and the air will be fresher all round. A few real supporters are always more important than many acquaintances. Think 80/20.

Q How you are going to use the 80/20 rule to improve your performance? Where is your 'sweet-spot'?

MESSAGE 33
DILIGENCE

Persist, act fast, go steady

Confucius, the Chinese philosopher who lived around 500 BC, said: 'The expectations of life depend upon diligence; the mechanic that would perfect his work must first sharpen his tools.'

The word 'diligence' is a powerful word. Be diligent. Work diligently. Diligent effort. Do due diligence. It has profound meaning and universal application. *Chambers Dictionary* defines the word diligent as an adjective meaning 'steady and earnest in application; industrious.'

The great writers and philosophers gave attention to the word. Dr. Samuel Johnson said: 'If your determination is fixed, I do not counsel you to despair. Few things are impossible to diligence and skill. Great works are performed

Your attitude rather than your aptitude determines your altitude. Recruit people first for their attitude. You can train them to acquire the necessary job skills

If at first you do succeed, try something more stretching which will facilitate you to become what you are capable of becoming

not by strength but by perseverance.'
Benjamin Franklin said: 'Diligence is
the mother of good luck.' Confucius
said, 'It does not matter how slowly
you go, as long as you do not stop.'

Persistence and diligence are used
interchangeably. Diligence is often
wrongly associated with getting things
done quickly. Persistence may mean
that you keep going steadily despite
boredom, despite personal mistakes,
despite adversity and despite success.

Get meaning and satisfaction from
implementing your current plan.
Without this, you won't have the
sustained energy and passion to
successfully take you through the
resistance points of your forward
journey.

Q The last time you
failed did you stop
trying because you
failed or did you
fail because you
stopped trying?

*Failure is only the
opportunity to
begin again more
intelligently*

Henry Ford

Perseverance is not
a long race; it is
many short races
one after another

Walter Elliott

Be diligent and
persevere. Try to keep
your feet on the
ground, your head
above the clouds, your
nose to the grindstone,
your shoulder to the
wheel, your finger on
the pulse, your eye on
the ball and your ear
to the ground

At times, you may have to act slowly and at other times, when the opportunity arises, you may have to act as quickly as you are able.

Adversity as the grindstone of life can either polish you up or grind you down. Which of these impacts it has on you depends on what you do with the difficulties that come your way.

The "middle way" as prescribed in Buddhism is a path between extremes. Good leaders and managers walk the path between extremes carefully and purposefully. They walk with diligence, they persist and they go steadily forward.

The highest reward for a person's toil is not what they get for it, but what they become by it

John Ruskin

Think about this ...

The six most important words

I admit that I was wrong

The five most important words

You did a great job

The four most important words

What do you think?

The three most important words

Could you please?

The two most important words

Thank you

The most important word

We

MESSAGE 34

NEGOTIATION

Speak clearly with courage
Listen with empathy

Alittle boy put his hand into a priceless flower vase and could not withdraw it. His mother, anxious to save her son's hand and also the vase, tried her best to get his hand out but failed. She said to him, "Open your hand, hold your fingers straight and then pull them out." To her astonishment her son said, "I can't pull my fingers out Mam because if I do I'll drop my penny." In negotiation, holding onto a penny can wrongly be perceived to be better than saving a hand or a priceless artefact.

Mahatma Gandhi, the charismatic leader of the independence movement for India in the 1920s, '30s and '40s practised non-violent social action and humanitarianism providing mankind with one of the greatest examples of the peaceful change that one individual can inspire. He not

The best deal of all is a triple win – a win for you, a win for the budgie and a win for me

Let us never negotiate out of fear but let us never fear to negotiate

John F. Kennedy

only proved the power of one person; he also proved that conflict can be resolved through negotiation.

Negotiation is the use by one party of power and of information to influence the behaviour of the other party. Negotiation is a form of influencing whereby you are trying to change the attitude and behaviour of the other party so that you can achieve your own goals. Communication in this process can be both the cause of conflict and the remedy for conflict. Silence is often the best form of communication.

Successful negotiation results in the disputing parties coming to an agreement about how they will behave toward one another. Conflict occurs when one or both parties are not able to secure what they need or want and are actively seeking their own goals. The conflict may be allowed to grow until it becomes too intense to resolve easily.

Never assume that you know what the other party wants. Understand that people are different and have different perspectives. You may feel drowned in

If two people agree on everything, you may be sure that just one of them is doing the thinking

Anyone who angers you, conquers you

Win the deal rather than the argument. Business is just another game

Know with whom you are negotiating. Do they have the authority?

It's easier to resist at the beginning than at the end

Leonardo da Vinci

information but starved of knowledge and capability. Get your facts first.

Good negotiators are good listeners. They look at people and then they look into them. One of the best ways of persuading others is by listening to them. You can understand them better. To understand is not necessarily to agree. One of the deepest needs of humans is to be understood. Listen with empathy.

If you are to become a successful negotiator, learn to control yourself. People who shout at each other will fail. Bullying tactics rarely succeed and exceptionally so, only if one party has enormous power. Yield to principles, but never yield to pressure. Know what you want from your negotiation. People who ask for more tend to get more.

One of the most important negotiation tactics is your 'walk-away' position. In negotiation you are only as free as your options, but make sure you have them worked out beforehand. Develop your BATNA – your Best Alternative To a Negotiated Agreement. Be prepared to do it.

The best outcome of any negotiation is that nobody loses face and everyone wins.

Timing is important. Delay is the coolest form of denial

I beg you to drop the trifle in your heart. Surrender! Let go and let God have His way in your life

Dr Billy Graham

No deal is preferable to a bad deal

Q Can you test your ability to listen without talking for as long as you can? Write down the result.

MESSAGE 35
MEDIATION

Compromise to win

There can be disagreement about ideas, information, theories, opinions and methods. There can be personality clashes. There can be business conflicts of interest. There can be historic differences between parents, partners, brothers, sisters and neighbours, some handed down from one generation to the next and successive generations thereafter. There can be disagreement about property, boundaries, inheritance, succession plans, marriage, money, politics, associations and friends. One or both parties, unable or unwilling to secure what they need or want by passive means set out to actively achieve it by aggressive means.

In conflict you may win the battle, but you may lose the war. Winning is not necessarily about victory over the opposition. Are you trying to expose someone for your own

When you wrestle with pigs, the pigs love it, but you get dirty

Forgive your enemies. It messes with their heads

Never does a man stand taller than when he foregoes revenge, and dares to forgive an injury

Edwin Hubbel Chapin

reasons? Do you want more out of your conflicts than a reasonable solution? Rather than looking back on retribution, focus forward to where your future is.

Eric Berne, M.D. author of *Games People Play*, set out the changes of behaviour that people exhibit. He says that at any given moment, each individual in a social aggregation will exhibit a Parental, an Adult or a Child ego state. In my experience as a mediator, I have seen people behave differently while in conflict and move between these different modes as they react to situations.

In Parental mode; everyone carries his or her parents around. You may act like your mother, when she wagged her finger at you. In Child mode, everyone carries around the little boy or girl they once were, inside of them. You may be spontaneous, excitable, petulant, difficult or disagreeable. In Adult mode, you may act rationally in a non-prejudicial manner. Before workable agreements can be reached, the mediator must bring the disputant parties into the Adult mode.

As organisations get flatter, management must rely less on power and more on influencing people. The workplace is a fertile breeding ground for conflicts because of the

Everybody can get angry, that's easy. But getting angry at the right person, with the right intensity, at the right time, for the right reason and in the right way, that's hard

Aristotle

Don't corner something meaner than you

Most litigation starts in anger and settles out of boredom

dynamics and inter-dependency of the various stakeholders. With so much time wasted in conflict this inevitably has a negative impact on productivity and on company morale.

Business contracts by their nature expect conflict. I firmly believe that arbitration and litigation are a last resort and that mediation between the parties in dispute should be tried and exhausted first. Before you think of litigation, try mediation. You may find it to be less expensive both psychologically and financially. Which do you want – victory or agreement? If you are patient in one moment of anger, you will escape a hundred days of sorrow.

A confident manager will be willing to bring his or her conflicts out into the open and prevent them from devouring his or her capacity to go forward. When you give oxygen to troubling issues they are fuelled. Take away that oxygen to reduce the grudges that are preventing you from great achievement. Take responsibility. Forgive the 'Other'. Move on with a light, determined step.

There is a thin line between being assertive and being aggressive. The methodology of the mediation process can achieve agreement between the most assertive and the most aggressive.

> If you argue and rankle and contradict you may achieve a victory sometimes but it will be an empty victory because you will never get your opponent's goodwill
>
> *Benjamin Franklin*

Q Can you think of a dispute you are familiar with in which mediation may be helpful?

We cannot solve problems by using the same kind of thinking we used when we created them. Mediation is a form of alternative dispute resolution (ADR) which facilitates new thinking. The focus of the mediation process is to facilitate the disputants to air their true interests and needs, not just their positions. It's trouble-shooting for common sense.

Mediation is not a court. The disputants are free to choose an outcome that is influenced as much by the future of their relationship, as their past conduct or conflict.

There is a myth of achieving justice from your "day in court". In reality, courts give you law, not justice. Courts have become the warehouse of disputes. They are adversarial. Instead, mediation is consensual.

The mediator facilitates the parties to listen empathically to the "other" side rather than listening with intent to reply. He or she facilitates the disputing parties to identify interests and not positions. They take the brave step to initiate discussion about the elephant in the room. Once you put the real issues on the table, they tend to be sorted quickly. It's impossible to solve issues which are kept under the table. Never assume that you know what the other party wants. Understand that people are different and have different perspectives on the negotiations. The mediation process facilitates the gradual de-layering of the symptoms which the dispute is presumed to be about and identifies the core issue.

Mediation with its focus on interests rather than positions, facilitates the disputants to go for a win-win type result rather than a win-lose. This will give longer-term benefits to all sides.

MESSAGE 36
TEAM

Engage all of us to be smarter than one of us

The boss of a company I visited was exasperated and exhausted. He could not understand why or how his company was losing out to the competition. I convinced him to gather his eight employees into a room, brainstorm the issues, divide the group into teams of four each, gave each team a task to identify the problems and come up with solutions.

Both teams came up with solutions that he had never dreamed of. Furthermore they committed themselves to outpacing the company's competitors. In a short space of time the company became number one in the market. He engaged each of the members of his staff and built a team that provided solutions.

The leader must use his/her relative power appropriately so that the planned outputs from the team can be achieved efficiently. They are quietly assertive in mobilizing the necessary resources and support to back their project and are not too concerned about who gets the credit

Gather the people you need to develop and deliver the vision or task or achieve the objective, seek their commitment to the task and give them deadlines by which it has to be done.

There is an old saying that a person who is his own doctor has a fool for a client. Think of your doctor, your accountant, your financial adviser, your solicitor, your car mechanic, your football coach as part of your personal development team. It is highly unlikely unless you are one of the world's few polymaths that you will be as smart as all of those specialists together and more so if they have had many years of tough and stretching experience.

Co-ops, credit unions, community groups and organisations are built on the concept of 'Ní neart go cur le chéile' – there is nothing we can't do if we work together. There is strength in unity. Few successes are achieved without the backing of a team. A family can become a hugely successful team if the family members override sibling rivalry or historical differences.

> Coming together is a beginning, staying together is progress and working together is success
>
> *Henry Ford*

Teams and groups satisfy people's emotional needs for affiliation, affection, warmth and self-worth. This structure facilitates synergy where the potential of the team is greater than the sum of its individual parts.

Planned output must be the core guiding principle you use when putting the team together. A winning team has effective and transparent communication processes. Everyone is crystal clear about the outputs of their respective roles.

As the team ages, "group think" tends to emerge. This can be both good and bad. The group can become corrupt. Emotions such as liking, affection, jealousy, anger, and hurt, can all grow in intensity. This may lead to a diluting of responsibility and objectivity. The reputation of the team can become more important than that of any individual. Consistency of procedures can become more important than whether or not it's the right thing to do.

If someone must be sacrificed for the perceived greater good of the team, so be it. A collection of individually brilliant people is often not as effective as a

> Individual commitment to a group effort – that is what makes a team work, a company work, a society work, a civilisation work
>
> *Vince Lombardi*

brilliant collection of minds that are focused on the agreed agenda.

When you are pulling a team or group together avoid elective homogeneity. The aggressor types will adopt bullying tactics in order to get their way. The ego trippers want to be heard and admired but make little contribution. Others will use political manipulation to get their way.

In any group of people, a small number will be leaders, a larger number will be followers and a substantial number won't want to get involved. The leader will gain respect from the others if he or she has clarity of purpose and capacity to convert their vision into a workable formula. Most people do not want glory hunters – they just want things to happen.

The greatest genius will not be worth much if he pretends to draw exclusively from his own resources

Johann Wolfgang von Goethe

Q Who among those you know would you have on your ten-member dream team to work with you on a business project?

MESSAGE 37
MARKETING

Convert niches into opportunities

A motor car provides transport. A mid-range motor car provides convenience and economy. A top-of-the-range motor car provides luxury and status. It may meet a need, a want and a demand. Perhaps the car in demand is a mobile office or a carrier for a disabled person. Perhaps it's a status statement. Perhaps it's a desired possession to satisfy an emotional want or to impress a peer group.

Good businesses apply scientific research to find out the needs, wants and demands of customers and potential customers. They know about humans and what you and I are thinking and they set out to answer it with a sale and with a relationship for life.

Behind an able man there are always other able men

Chinese Proverb

First find the niche in the market and having found it, satisfy the market in the niche

Anon

The smart decision-makers of major, small and medium enterprises are customer-obsessed. They know it would be impossible to satisfy everybody. That's why they focus on satisfying segments of the market with their best service.

They try to convert niches into opportunities. They completely satisfy one niche and then try to fill another. They kill off the competition and keep the customer. That's marketing.

Marketing is about customers. That's it. No more and no less. Its objective is simple: satisfy customers' needs, wants and demands right now. Give customers an experience in which they will buy your products or services and keep on buying them.

Q Is there a need for your talent, your product or your service, in your village, town or community? Can you charge for it?

Think about this ...

Procter and Gamble

In 1879, Procter and Gamble's best seller was candles. The company was in trouble, however. Thomas Edison had invented the light bulb and it looked as if candles would become obsolete. By mistake one operator forgot to turn off his machine when he went to lunch. When he came back a frothing mass of lather filled with air bubbles was around the machine. He almost threw the stuff away but instead decided to make it into soap. The soap floated. Thus, Ivory soap was born and became the mainstay of the Procter and Gamble Company.

MESSAGE 38
SELLING

Dominate with listening

Listen. Everybody is selling something whether it is a product, a service, a personal promise or gossip. Every discussion is a trading situation whether of experiences, knowledge or social interaction. Every relationship between people is a marketplace.

The skill of listening is probably the most important negotiation skill in that marketplace whether it is in talking with a friend or asking someone to buy something from you.

Good customer service is the cheapest form of promotion. It's an attitude. If you don't take care of your customers, someone else will

If you are not serving the end customer, you have to be serving someone who is

Jan Carlzo

The reason a dog has so many friends is that his tail wags instead of his tongue

If you cannot smile, you should not keep a shop

Listen actively and attentively to what the other person is saying. In that way you will be able to identify the person's needs and wants and fill them accurately and completely. It's the art of common courtesy.

Listen also to what the person is NOT saying. In that way you will be able to ascertain what conditions the person wants for receiving and accepting what you are saying, what you are offering, what you are asking, what you are selling. Listen long and hard. It's the bedrock of selling and negotiating.

When your customer buys a product or service from you, they are actually hiring you to solve an issue relevant to them at that moment. Never forget

Q What would it be like to be a customer dealing with your business?

You can make more friends in two months by becoming more interested in other people than you can in two years of trying to get people interested in you

Good listening skills are the bedrock for effective communication and thus selling. Active listening means being engaged with your potential customer, trying to understand their needs and wants

Someone trying to sell a blind horse always praises its feet

German proverb

that your potential customer is selfish for their own agendas, not yours. How they perceive your proposition is the real motivator for them.

Assuming your range of marketing interventions is working, you have physically positioned yourself within the four-foot space of your targeted customer. This is where your selling skills come into play. To understand customers' wants is a great step towards influencing them to buy. Diagnose before you prescribe. Listen.

If you cannot meet your customer's initial demands, change their expectations. Condition them so that you can better manage their expectations

The buyer needs a hundred eyes; the seller but one

Italian proverb

Nature gave us one tongue and two ears so we could hear twice as much as we speak

Epictetus

A professional does his best at a time when he doesn't particularly feel like it

MESSAGE 39
MEASUREMENT

Calculate with care

One of the most important decisions you will make for managing your personal life, your home life, or your business, is to measure what you are doing.

Benchmarks against which to measure your progress are time spent, time saved, time to spend on other things, money spent, money saved, money gained, energy spent, and energy saved and so on.

How much time will I need to get to the airport? How much money will I need to afford the standard of living and the lifestyle I like?

If you don't have a clearly defined benchmark against which to judge progress you can never be accused of not achieving. This, in itself, is a comfort-zone. It is not a very productive one.

What gets measured tends to get done.

By measuring according to your benchmarks and indicators you are giving a clear signal to those around you which outputs are most important to you. Generally, they will be directly influenced by your agenda.

Output is the metric which the market uses to calculate your remuneration. Thus, it must be the metric by which you judge yourself and your team.

There is nothing as unequal as the equal treatment of unequals.

Q (i) What are you currently measuring in your business?

(ii) Are these the critical issues you should be measuring?

MESSAGE 40

POLITICS

Manage the art of survival

The politician looks to the next general election while a statesman looks to the next generation. Everybody could learn from professional politicians and how they survive and achieve what they achieve despite formidable competition.

Most professional politicians have noble ambitions to do great good for their constituents and country by improving the lives and living standards of people. However, the political system inhibits that ambition and politics intervenes on good economic management. Scarce resources are spent with both eyes on winning the next election. It's the art of survival.

People elect politicians based on many subjective criteria such as clientelism or cronyism. Competence to do the job may not be foremost in their consideration. Politicians are basically mandated to defend the interests of

It is better to be hated for what one is, than loved for what one is not

Andre Gide

Q What do you stand for?

three aspects of the nation – economic, legal and health. Governments do not create jobs. Good governments create the environment in which sustainable jobs can best be created.

Opposition politicians are experts on what has to be done. When in power, they become expert at articulating reasons why it can't be done. They do whatever it takes to survive. The memories of the electorate are short. US President Bill Clinton once wisely and succinctly summed up politics: 'It's the economy, stupid.' The electorate are pacified when the money is rolling in. People everywhere are pacified when they have money that gives them a feeling of security and comfort.

The art of politics as performed by professional politicians is mirrored in the games that people play in their own lives. Ordinary people can learn the use of scarce resources from the masters of negotiation, planning and compromise. It's the art of survival.

There is nothing as easy as denouncing. It doesn't take much to see that something is wrong, but it takes vision to see that it will be put right again.

The politician who smiles when things go wrong has thought out who he will blame for it.

It's hard to believe that a man is telling the truth when you know that you would lie if you were in his place.

I know what you are against, but I don't know what you are for

Anon

Money Management

Creating wealth from scarce resources

MESSAGE 41
INVESTMENTS

Be risk-averse

Grandad Number One said: 'Never keep all your eggs in one basket'. Grandad Number Two said: 'Invest no more than you can afford to lose'. For a deeper understanding of investment, I turned to Grandad Number One who had gone through hard times, built a small business and went to Las Vegas for a week every year. He said investment is like working the one-armed bandit in the corner of the casino: 'You buy, you hold, you sell but knowing when to sell and buy depends on years of coming to Las Vegas'.

My Grandad Number Two who was a farmer said it's like farming: 'It depends on the weather and it depends on the fertiliser and management. When you sow a field of corn, some seedlings die, some stay small, but most grow'.

The essence of investment is to give up some small current resources to make larger quantities of future resources

I learned to do without before I learned to enjoy
Niccolo Machiavelli

No one was ever ruined by taking a profit
Stock Exchange maxim

My friend, an economist, said: 'Hold onto everything you have, put it in a safe and you will one day be able to afford bargains that nobody else can'.

Some investors gain enormously and make "a killing" whether the stock market is moving up or moving down. Investments are a risk to get future reward. The world's economies would collapse without investors. Investors contribute to economic growth and to jobs.

The conundrum that continues to baffle people is how to invest to be sure of a 'reasonable' return. The answer is that there is no certainty. Values can go up or down. Booms may give good and bad returns on investment. Downturns in the economy can also give good returns if you know what you are doing. A rumour of poor performance may result in collapse of shares and stocks and whole businesses and whole countries. Pension Funds have collapsed and they have risen exponentially.

Techniques, such as ratio analysis can help you to get a third-dimensional view of business investment. If you already have financial freedom and are debt-free

If you don't sow seed in the spring time, you won't reap at the harvest time

The trouble with getting something right first time is that nobody appreciates how difficult it was to achieve

The markets can stay irrational a lot longer than you can stay solvent

John Maynard Keynes

No price is too low for a bear or too high for a bull

Stock Exchange Proverb

you may spend your time in having fun, doing a training course, enjoying a sport, meeting with friends, and taking no more risk.

Investment can come from a number of possible sources. However, it will probably come from:

(a) surplus money that you can afford to invest or

(b) Other People's Money (OPMs) – that is from people who want to invest in your dream.

Generally it will be some combination of these. In order to have a surplus from your own resources, you need more funds coming in rather than going out.

If and when you become debt-free and achieve financial freedom, your next challenge is to hold on to what you have achieved. What would your Grandads say?

Q How diversified is your investment plan?

Cut your losses and let your profits run

American proverb

The markets are fuelled by rumours to which the herd responds. Become a contrarian and avoid the herd

Be able to give up at any given moment all that we are for what we can become

W.E.B. De Bois, American Civil Rights leader

Know your worth. People tend to over-value what they are not and undervalue what they are

MONEY

Turn cash-flow into happiness

You are swimming in a beautiful pool having the time of your life and someone pulls the plug. That's a metaphor for the effect of negative cash-flow. There's lots of water in the tank and there's more to flow into the pipeline but just at the time you need it, there's no water there in the swimming pool to swim in.

The management of cash-flow is a vital skill in making money go round and be available when you need it. Whether you are a homemaker or

Market commentators work on probability. When making your judgement calls about your wealth, ignore what they say

It's good to have money and the things that money can buy but check once in a while to make sure that you haven't lost the things that money can't buy

Prosperity is a good teacher; adversity is a greater one

the president of a multinational business, you will at one time have cash-flow challenges when you have too little money to keep going, at another time just enough to get by and another time when you have too much money and are undecided what to do with it.

Cash-flow crises happen to children, to employees and to business people every day, every week, every month of the year. How to achieve a continuously positive, balanced cash-flow is a combination of management effort, creativity, prudence, art and science. Seasonal workers such as those working in tourism may have an income for only three months of the year. How will they use that income for the rest of the year? Tillage farmers may not get paid for their crops until the end of the year. How are they going to live, support their families and invest in future development for the next season?

Accountants look back to see how you have spent money in the past. Then they look forward to see how you might spend in the future. You may have valuable assets such as a house, a car, a holiday home and investments but you

It is easy to get the things you want, provided you first learn to do without the things you cannot get

Happiness is a positive cash flow

Fred Adler, venture capitalist

The road from €10m to €1m is not as pleasant as the road from €0 to €1m

Money can't buy happiness; it can, however, rent it

Profit is an illusion; cash-flow is fact

may have little or no liquid cash to live on or to develop.

If you want to move forward, you will base your economic decisions on how to assess future cash flows. Consider your job or your business as a cash-generating machine. When cash is coming in, you have cash inflow, when cash is being spent, you have cash outflow. This may happen in fluctuations of the values of creditors, debtors, capital, reserves, and stocks.

Open a spreadsheet, estimate your living expenses and future cash flow and build on it to increase your wealth towards financial freedom and a state of happiness.

Q What have you learned from the economic depression?

The moment of victory is much too short to live for and nothing else

Martina Navratilova

It is only the poor who pay cash and that's not from virtue but because they are refused credit

Anatole France

Money is like an arm or leg – use it or lose it

Henry Ford 1931

The two most beautiful words in the English language are "cheque enclosed"

Dorothy Parker

MESSAGE 43
TAXES

Pay up for society

Open your salary or wage packet to see that gross is so much and that thirty per cent or more is taken in taxes by Government. Taxes are the only means through which society pays for the services that keep it going.

We all need taxes to keep us in the relative comfort that we have at present. Taxes are necessary to create the environment or climate in which to preserve and grow businesses and create more jobs, pay for pensions, social welfare, raise the standards of living and the quality of life so that everyone gains.

Entrepreneurs and their businesses generate income and growth and jobs. Governments use taxes on businesses and on employees to pay for the services that keep whole countries alive. Governments

There is one difference between a tax collector and a taxidermist – the taxidermist leaves the hide
Mortimer Caplan

Tax has made more liars out of the American people than golf
Will Rogers

We don't pay taxes. The little people pay taxes
Leona Helmsley

use taxes as levers to incentivize people's behaviours or to change policies.

Governments often increase or decrease taxes to encourage growth or spending or to manage debt. Their decisions are often manipulative for political purposes. They may ignore the advice of advisory bodies and economists for political purposes. That is why people must question politicians continually on the distribution and fairness of taxes. Such criticism will help Governments and Government agencies to improve their services.

Many individuals and businesses too may be missing out on the tax breaks or allowances due to them. That is why every taxpayer, every business owner, should know what entitlements they have. They may be losing large amounts of money because of their failure to take their entitlements that, in turn, lead to increased standards of living and investments in the local economy and society.

There is just one thing I can promise you about the outer-space programme, your tax-dollar will go further

Werner von Braun

The art of taxation consists in so plucking the goose as to obtain the largest amount of feathers with the least possible amount of hissing

J. B. Colbert

Q Are we getting a fair return for the taxes we are paying?

Future growth outcomes

Happiness is a life well lived and a good legacy

MESSAGE 44
MATURITY

Respond to life's challenges

Young people may have maturity beyond their years while older people may lack the indefinable quality of maturity. It is difficult to define the psychological characteristic or attribute of maturity adequately. A description of maturity in action may be how to act, react and make decisions that lead to the best possible outcomes in challenging situations.

Synonyms for maturity include readiness, ability, experience, capability, perfection, completion, fitness, wisdom. Antonyms include ignorance, impotence, inability, incompetence, stupidity. Will readiness, ability, experience, capability, completion, fitness and wisdom prepare us for life's challenges?

Do we make decisions based on the optimum money to be made or do we make them

In the absence of a great dream, pettiness prevails

Maturity is letting life happen in its own good order, and making the most of what there is. Maturity is being smarter at managing the variables you have control over

based on the best outcome for our family, friends and neighbours? Or, do we make decisions based on the best outcomes for ourselves? Are they for self-preservation or to have a good time?

Is maturity innate wisdom? Is it a combination of experience, wisdom, culture or just common sense? Is it a way of acting?

A mature person will be able to tolerate certain pain, laugh, engage in social interaction, decide what is important and unimportant, be optimistic, be competent, and have a good outlook and philosophy on life. Your definition and understanding of maturity is as good as any other. Be yourself.

Q If you had nothing to fear, what would you do right now?

Your home is your refuge. Keep only cheerful friends

Experience is the name everyone gives to their mistakes

Oscar Wilde

Think about this ...

Prayer of St Francis Assisi

Lord, make me an instrument of your peace,

Where there is hatred, let me sow love

Where there is injury, pardon

Where there is doubt, faith

Where there is despair, hope

Where there is darkness, light

And where there is sadness, joy.

MESSAGE 45
NEXT STEP

Climb more hills

The film *Shawshank Redemption*, one of the most popular films of all time, features Andy Dufresne (Tim Robbins), in prison for nineteen years for a murder he didn't commit. He said to his fellow inmate, Red Redding (Morgan Freeman): 'I guess it comes down to a simple choice, really. Get busy living or get busy dying.' He got busy living.

Catholics, Buddhists, Hindus, all believe that there is a follow-on life after this life on earth. If you are an atheist or agnostic, you have no need to worry either – if death is the end, well that's it. If life is everlasting change, death is a mere change to another form of life. If all that exists are energy and matter, death is a mere transformation.

Death is a natural part of the life process. It's merely the end of life as you'll know it.

What a wonderful life I have had. If only I had realised it sooner. All my life I wanted to be someone else but I failed to decide who

He who has a "Why?" to live for, can bear almost any "How?"

Write the epitaph that you would like to have on your tombstone

Fear of death will achieve nothing.

Bereaved people of a generation ago became pre-occupied with rituals and remembrances that paralysed them or suspended the lives of remaining family and friends from moving on and living their own lives. It is natural to feel sadness at the passing of a loved one. However, prolonged focus on death and on what remains, is unhealthy. In some cases, it reaches a stage of overwhelming grief and requires medical or psychological help.

With today's medicine, medical and nursing help for those who are in pain or have a terminal illness, the transformation from here to a hereafter is eased and, in many cases, pain-free.

Try to keep thoughts of death to a minimum. Focus instead on thoughts of living and doing.

Billions of people have died before you and billions more will die after you. Many of those will have died

I am ready to meet my Maker. Whether my Maker is prepared for the great ordeal of meeting me is another matter

Winston Churchill

Don't wait until it's too late to say sorry for some outstanding misunderstanding or to say: "I really love and appreciate you"

What difference does it make to the dead, the orphans and the homeless, whether the mad destruction is wrought under the name of totalitarianism or the holy name of liberty or democracy?

Mahatma Gandhi

in their youth or will not have lived life into old age. Don't worry about the loss of your freedom or dignity in old age. If all else has failed due to old age, use your imagination.

There is, of course, the possibility that in future, worn out body parts will be replaced and each person will live on this Earth part biological body and part machine for hundreds of years or perhaps forever.

Think of what you would most like to do for yourself or for others while you are alive

Q Where are you going this week?

Live in day-tight compartments. Ask yourself, what is the worst that can possibly happen, prepare to accept the worst, try to improve on the worst

Dale Carnegie

Dúirt mé leat go raibh mé breoite (I told you I was ill) Love, light, peace

Spike Milligan

These then are my last words to you: Be not afraid of life. Believe that life is worth living, and your belief will help create the fact

William James

MESSAGE 46
LEGACY

Leave this place better-off

Moss Cass, Australian minister for the environment and conservation, so profoundly said to the OECD in Paris in 1974: 'We, rich nations, for that is what we are, have an obligation not only to the poor nations but to all the grandchildren of the world, rich and poor. We have not inherited this earth from our parents to do with it what we will. We have

Make your will if you have not already done so. If you have already made your will, consider updating it. The process will clarify your assets and help you clarify your future. You'll live better when you've made a will

Leave something small to someone outside of your family and close friends

Make your own funeral arrangements

Facilitate your followers to have a goal which they can automatically have a passion to go after with the enthusiasm of a child and the head of a mature person

borrowed it from our children and we must be careful to use it in their interests as well as our own. Anyone who fails to recognise the basic validity of the proposition put in different ways by increasing numbers of writers, from Malthus to The Club of Rome, is either ignorant, a fool, or evil.'

You are passing through this world but once. Any good that you can do, do it now for you will not pass this way again. Use your capacity to encourage others to be more successful than you.

Empathise with people who are down on their luck. Help them to help themselves. They are looking at the world from the inside out. You are looking at their world from the outside in. Effective interventions are reflective of inside-out perspectives. One day they may become materially wealthy again. One day, they may give you the hand-up or the hand-out you want.

Q What non-material legacy do you plan to leave after you?

What footprint do you want to leave after you on your forward journey?

Leave this place a little better than you found it

Baden Powell

Humans are resilient and the survival instinct is strong in all of us

What do you want to be remembered for?

The great use of life is to spend it for something that will outlast it

William James

What difference do you want to make?

It is preoccupation with possession, more than anything else that prevents men from living freely and nobly

Bertrand Russell

Success has many sponsors. Failure has none

Think about this ...

The Best

If you can't be a pine on top of the hill
Be a scrub in the valley – but be
The best little scrub at the side of the rill.
Be a bush if you can't be a tree.

If you can't be a bush, be a bit of grass
Some highway to happier make.
If you can't be a muskie then just be a bass,
But the liveliest bass in the lake.

We can't all be captains, we've got to have crew,
There's something for all of us here.
There's big work to do and there's lesser work too
And the task we must do is near.

If you can't be a highway, then just be a trail.
If you can't be the sun be a star.
It isn't by size that you win or you fail.
Be the best of whatever you are.

MESSAGE 47
LESSONS

Learn from everything

Pat Lambert was aged thirty when he inherited the small family farm of thirty acres from his father. By age forty, he had acquired the equivalent of fourteen times the size of his small farm. Members of the community admired his meteoric rise from poverty to millions. It was millions created from bank borrowing.

By aged forty-five, Pat was bankrupt. His life was in tatters. His bankruptcy made newspaper headlines. The once admiring people shunned him. Pat told me that bankruptcy with all its pain and embarrassment was the best thing that ever happened to him. He learned more lessons from the experience than he could from the lessons of several lifetimes. By aged sixty, he was a multimillionaire again. This time in reality. He had applied the harsh lessons he had learned.

Never test the depth of the water with both feet

Take responsibility for your choices to liberate yourself from the conditioning inputs of your life journey

Misery arises when we want something we can't have

Edwin Barnes, no money and little education, visualized that one day he would work with Thomas Edison, inventor of the phonograph, the movie camera and the electric light bulb. Many inspirational quotes are attributed to Edison. His most famous are: 'I have not failed. I've just found 10,000 ways that won't work.' 'Many of life's failures are people who did not realise how close they were to success when they gave up.' 'We often miss opportunity because it's dressed in overalls and looks like work.' 'Genius is one per cent inspiration and ninety-nine per cent perspiration.'

Barnes did not want to work for Edison. He wanted to learn from him. They formed a partnership and succeeded.

Success in life is all about learning lessons. Success gives lessons that will teach you about failure. Failure gives lessons to help you achieve success.

> The only man who never makes a mistake is the man who never does anything
>
> *Theodore Roosevelt*

> I never knew a person who suffered from overwork. There are many, however, who suffered from too much ambition, and not enough action
>
> *Dr James Mantague*

> *The road to success is lined with many tempting parking spaces*

Business researchers today say that you cannot have success without having had several failures. In Ireland, up to recent times, society disowned failures. In the US, investors will not invest in your project unless they know that you have failed several times.

Those who succeed are those who keep going and learning from each expensive lesson. The expense will hopefully not be so much that you lose everything. Your priority should be to first protect your home and your base income. If you invest money, can you afford to lose it all?

Success is not so much a question of ability as a question of application of the lessons you learn. Manage money pragmatically – in your head rather than in your heart.

Be a contrarian. Avoid the herd. Make yourself a reputation for being a creative genius; surround yourself with partners who are better than you. The secret to the future is how you act in the present. Improve on the present and the future will improve.

Recall the lessons that you have learned and turned to your advantage. Recall

Learn to enjoy every minute of your life. Be happy now. Don't wait for something outside of yourself to make you happy in the future. Think how really precious is the time you have to spend, whether it's at work or with your family. Every minute should be enjoyed and savoured

Earl Nightingale

If you are making mistakes make sure they are new ones

Behold the turtle; he makes progress only when he sticks his neck out

Bruce Levin

people who taught you the most valuable lessons regardless of whether you liked them? All genuine knowledge originates in our reactions to our experiences.

Our deepest urge is to be important and to be appreciated and liked. The desire to be important has driven all the great achievements.

Taking responsibility for your choices is the only way you can liberate yourself from the conditioning inputs of your life journey to date.

The trouble with many of us is that in trying times we stop trying. Achievement and success are not so much about ability as application of the lessons you learn.

Nothing is over until the moment you stop trying.

A lifetime of happiness! No man alive could bear it: it would be hell on earth

G.B. Shaw

Success is how high you bounce when you hit the bottom

Each one of us occupies a vital patch in the tapestry of life. We are influenced and we are influencers. Let's be positive influencers in our own patch

What the wise do at the beginning the foolish do at the end. Avoid the herd instinct

Epilogue

Seven life messages

The 47 core messages in this book can be distilled into seven major messages. If you apply these messages, they will have a profound effect on your life and living.

1. Change

Each of us is born with a genetic map. It's our DNA. We can't change it. However we can change our approach to living and to the events we encounter on our life's journey. Then we can begin to make it better. Change is good for us.

2. Stand out from the crowd

While growing up, the middle ground was considered to be the safe space. If we stood out from the crowd or the herd as it is often called we were likely to be penalized.

The crowd was generally a bigger influence on our lives as we became part of the club or gang or peer group. We became socialized. We discovered along life's journey that the crowd is not always right and most often is wrong. Stand out from the crowd. Become a contrarian.

3. Grow a team of supporters

We can't choose the family or circumstances we were born into. But we can choose our new extended network of people with whom we connect. We need to develop our own circle of friends, our own team of like-minded associates, our own network of genuine supporters. We can't do everything on our own. We also need to build some identity capital – a reputation for good with our network. If we know where we are going, we will always attract the required support. We cannot help those who don't know where they want to get to.

4. Give quality input to gain quality output

We cannot get out what we don't put in. Life is an input/output model. The quality of our input is the biggest contributor to our output. However, we mustn't allow ourselves to be defined by what we haven't already done. The past is gone – what matters is what we do with the time that remains.

5. Seek clarity

We must have more clarity about where we are right now and the various staging posts to get to our desired destination. How can you know what path to take if you are in the midst of a fog? Shout out for clarity.

6. Pay the price

Everything in life has a price and we must consciously or sub-consciously decide if we are prepared to pay this price. The price may be time or money or resources or our personal commitment. Are you prepared to pay the price right now? Or, are you prepared to defer that payment?

7. Nibble forward

One of the most powerful and most useful words in the English language is the word 'nibble'. It means to bite gently in small bites. It means eat a little bit at a time.

Applied to living life, no matter what problem or challenge is daunting you or preventing you from moving forward, nibble at it but do so in a forward direction towards your goal. You'll be amazed at the effect that a nibble forward has on a major challenge or problem.

Finally

To get the most value from this book, pick out one or two messages. Then try to understand the messages in a practical way. Next agree an action plan with yourself and execute the plan. Then enjoy the output or outcome.

In turn talk about what you have learned and share it with others for their benefit.

Nibble in a forward direction at the challenges you face to reveal the interesting opportunities that life presents to you.

I dare you.

The 47 phenomenon

The number 47 is significant in my life. It has featured so many times, it's uncanny. Is it synchronicity, is it serendipity or is it just chance?

When compiling this collection of messages, I found that the result was 47. That coincides with a series of 47s in my life.

The number is used many times in Star Wars, Mars has a 47 year cycle and 1947 was the 47th US Open. The US Declaration of Independence has 47 sentences. There are 47 strings on a concert harp.

Or is it because the world's most popular number, the so called lucky number 7, is part of it. There are 7 days in the week, 7 basic music notes and 7 ancient wonders of the world.

Some people told me that 47 contains three 7s. If you look at the 4 in 47, it contains two 7s, one atop the other.

Perhaps you have similar experience with numbers. Perhaps I'm just lucky!

Bibliography

An Unsung Hero: Tom Crean – Antarctic Survivor by Michael Smith

Essai sur la Nature du Commerce en Général (Essay on the Nature of Commerce) by Richard Cantillon

The Practice of Management by Peter Drucker

The Second Curve by Charles Handy

Designing for Growth by Liedka and Olgilvie

Business Model Generation by Osterwalder and Pigneur

Who Moved my Cheese by Spencer Johnson

The Black Swan by Nassim Nicholas Taleb

Time to Think by Nancy Kline

Thinking Fast and Slow by Daniel Kahneman

That'll Never Work by Michael Gaffney and Colin O'Brien

Breaking Bread by Brody Sweeney

The Secret by Rhonda Byrne

Think and Grow Rich by Napoleon Hill

The Richest man in Babylon by George Samuel Clason

A History of Christianity by Diarmuid McCulloch

A Book of Hours by Thomas Merton

The Power of Now by Eckhart Tolle

The Monk who sold his Ferrari by Robin Sharma.

GOD GAVE YOU A LICENCE
TO BECOME WHAT YOU
WANT MOST TO BECOME.

YOU ARE MUCH
GREATER THAN
YOU THINK YOU ARE.